ASHMOLEAN

Japanese Decorative Arts of the Meiji Period 1868–1912

OLIVER IMPEY
AND
JOYCE SEAMAN

Ashmolean Museum,
2005

First published in the United Kingdom in 2005 by the Ashmolean Museum, Publications Department, Beaumont Street, Oxford OX1 2PH

ISBN 1 85444 197 3 (hardback)
ISBN 1 85444 198 1 (hardback)

Titles in this series include:
Ruskin's Drawings
Worcester Porcelain
Maiolica
Drawings by Michelangelo and Raphael
Oxford and the Pre-Raphaelites
Islamic Ceramics
English Embroideries
Indian Paintings from Oxford collections
Camille Pissarro and his family
Eighteenth-century French porcelain
Miniatures
Samuel Palmer
Twentieth-century paintings
Ancient Greek pottery
English Delftware
J.M.W. Turner
Glass of four millennia
Finger rings
Frames and framing
French drawings and watercolours
Scythian and Thracian antiquities

British Library Cataloguing in Publication Data
A catalogue record for this book is available from the British Library

Designed and typeset in Garamond and Frutiger by Rhian Lonergan-White, Ashmolean Museum.
Printed by Craft Print, Singapore

The Ashmolean

Contents

Preface

Until 1987, the Department of Eastern Art of the Ashmolean had not sought to acquire decorative works of art from Japan of the second half of the nineteenth century and the first decades of the twentieth. These were very much out of fashion in museum circles, though there were by then several serious private collectors both in America and in England. In fact, the British Museum had acquired a pair of Imperial presentation cloisonné vases by Namikawa Sōsuke in the mid eighties, perhaps as much for their historical interest as for themselves; nevertheless, the British Museum actively bought them. The Victoria and Albert had acquired excellent examples of Meiji art-crafts before the end of the Meiji period, but thereafter collected almost nothing.

The Department held a few pieces of the period, some of them extremely fine, and ten of these are included in this catalogue. Several of these are recorded as having been purchased in Japan by Sir Herbert and Lady Ingram on their honeymoon in Japan in 1908; this group is being studied by Joyce Seaman. The art market provided the opportunity for purchase, the leading specialist being Malcolm Fairley then of Sotheby's, and it was with his encouragement that the first purchase was made, the Andō cloisonné vase (No. 39). As far as we are aware, no other museum in Britain or continental Europe, and possibly none in America or Japan was active in this field until some years later.

In 1991 the department held one of the first exhibitions of Meiji period decorative art since the period; the inclusion of the Shibayama style pieces was certainly the first museum exhibition of the style anywhere, since the pieces were new. This was the collection of John R. Young, of Texas, and was published by Impey and Fairley as 'The Dragon King of the Sea'. Collaboration with Fairley over the publication of the great collection of Dr David Khalili gave Impey more exposure to Meiji art, and the collection started to grow by active purchase, made possible by use of the fund left to us by Jeffery Story. Obviously the field is a large one and we have had to specialize; we have acquired examples by certain of the finer artists, e.g. Namikawa Yasuyuki and Makuzu Kōzan in preference to others, in order to be able to trace the evolution of their styles and hence to extrapolate to the work of other artists.

We have tried hard only to acquire works of the finest quality, even with the limited budget available to us, and the viewer will find some minor (or even major) masterpieces. We hope to continue to add to the collection.

Regrettably, for reasons of conservation the textiles are rarely on display.

January 2004.

'Art-crafts' of Meiji Period Japan

Oliver Impey

It is not easy to overstate the cataclysmic effects of the run-up to the implementation of the Meiji 'Restoration' in Japan in 1868. An analogy might be the change from the Communist regime in Russia and Eastern Europe to the so-called free market of the west. The change affected every aspect of Japanese life; a new sense of a single nation, as opposed to a series of regional loyalties, was created; a constitution was written; land reform, education reform, reform of the justice system, transport, almost every aspect of Japanese life was radically altered, much of it closely adhering to western models. It was a triumph for the new ruling oligarchy that it succeeded.

It was not really a 'restoration'; the Emperor remained the titular head of the nation, deeply revered and almost worshipped, but was in effect a constitutional monarch under a parliamentary system instead of under the Tokugawa Shoguns. The word Meiji means 'enlightened government', and the new government had as a primary aim the bringing of Japan into the group of the modern western industrial powers. It was essential to gain parity with the west in order to renegotiate the 'Unequal Treaties' imposed upon Japan by the western nations in the 1850s.

One of the ways the government decided to do this was to demonstrate to the world the brilliance of Japanese craftsmanship through the media of the International Industrial Expositions that were such a feature of the second half of the nineteenth century and the first two decades of the twentieth. The legacy of craftsmanship of the Edo period (1600–1868) was vital to this; it was not so much the craftsmanship that changed as the clientele. Craftsmen had to adapt to a totally new demand, a demand from the west for new concepts in shape and decoration which must have been more than alien to them. Earlier Japanese visitors to Europe had noted the love of decoration of the time; High Victorianism. Naturally, craftsmen attempted to cater to such a perceived demand, and early Meiji exhibition pieces do tend to look as if they were designed by a committee: they often were. But for Japan this was a revelation; this was new; this was the future.

The first International Exposition to which the Japanese contributed was that in Paris in 1867. To this, two independent clans, the Satsuma and the Saga contributed as well as the Tokugawa Government itself; significantly, the Victoria and Albert Museum made most of their purchases from the Satsuma stand. It was not until the Vienna exposition of 1873 that the Japanese scored a major success; this, of course, was after the 'restoration' and the new government actively encouraged the promotion of the sale of Japanese art-crafts' by the setting up of the Kiriu Kōshō Kaisha (First Trading and Manufacturing

Company) [the first word used to be read Kiritsu, but Kiriu is now known to be correct.] This company provided designs by painters, often in the late Edo version of the Rimpa style, for craftsmen in other materials to convert into metalwork and other materials, often, of course, on rounded as opposed to flat shapes. To some extent this fossilized these crafts, and many craftsmen failed to notice the dramatic changes in western taste that were occurring at the end of the nineteenth century.

Other companies, such as the Ōzeki Company, or the Maruki Company, were set up privately or with government help; certainly with government encouragement. These companies were entrepreneurs in the commissioning of works of craft of high quality from well-known craftsmen and exhibiting them under (and even inscribing them with) their own names as opposed to the names of the craftsmen who actually made them. In the five National Industrial Expositions of the Meiji period, held in the years that avoided any international exposition, and which were, like the latter, competitive (a new idea, like many others, in Japan), it was the commissioning companies that won the major prizes; the actual makers won lesser prizes. This points directly to the agenda of the government; to get these things made for exhibition for the good name of Japan.

This top-of-the-range craftsmanship must be distinguished from the mass of inferior goods that the Japanese, rightly assessing the lower ends of the market, poured into Europe and America. Usually there is no problem; one can instantly detect the difference between the bad and the good. What is more difficult is to detect the difference between the good and the very good. Herbert Ponting (published in 1910) recounts how he visited the celebrated metalworker Kuroda Kiichi in Kyōto: shown some of his work, Ponting praised it, whereupon Kuroda deprecated it and showed him what he and his discerning Japanese clients (for there was a good internal market for the best modern work, too) would regard as good enough; there was a distinct difference which Ponting could only then see.

During the Edo period most craftsmen had either worked for a 'feudal' lord, or a *diamyō*, or had worked for the newly rich townsmen or merchants, the *chōnin*. In the former case, the best example would be the makers of sword-fittings, the *tsuba* and other accoutrements of the all-important pair of swords worn by every samurai. For such a craftsman, and there was a group in every regional centre of Japan, working for their local *daimyō*, the lord would have provided the workshop and the material, had a strong influence on the output and acquired the final result; after the law banning the wearing of swords in 1876 (surprisingly late), such craftsmen had perforce to become independent, to purchase their own raw materials and to make something saleable in a new and radically different market.

The ceramics of the Meiji period were as innovative as and much more varied than those of any previous time in Japan. One has only to think of the 'brocaded' Satsuma decorated wares, which arose at the beginning of Meiji, to be aware that there was much new work.

Admittedly the Satsuma wares depend on Kyōto pottery for inspiration, but they rapidly developed their own various identities even though they were made in a number of different areas of Japan. There has been much argument about the origin of the Satsuma wares and when they first began, but it seems clear now that they came from the Kagoshima kilns of the Satsuma Daimyō in Kyushu, in the middle of the nineteenth century. The innumerable so-called Satsuma factories varied widely in both methods and results; for our purposes here we can point to three factories. The Kyōto factory of Kinkōzan Sōbei, set up inn the middle Edo period, begun to specialise in high quality Satsuma type wares early in the Meiji period, employing good potters and fine individual painters, usually decorating in the fine scale more or less characteristic of any so-called Satsuma. See the dish (no.18) for this fine style; see also the *art nouveau* vase of only a few years later, showing how Kinkōzan responded to the developing taste of the west.

Yabu Meizan, on the other hand, was a decorator; blanks were imported, probably from Kagoshima and decorated in one of his two characteristic styles. The earlier style employed the use of stencils simply to outline the placing of the innumerable small figures that were his speciality (though he often used flowers, too); these would then be painted extremely finely in great detail. Frequently the figures formed a procession; the collection lacks such a piece. In 1910, at the time of the Japan-British Exposition at Shepherd's Bush, he introduced a new, open style on a larger scale, where the design complemented the shape of the vessel, and the painting was an up-to-date version of the Shijō style, not unlike the style of Watanabe Seitei, a painter who provided designs for the cloisonné of Namikawa Sōsuke (See nos. 44 and 46). For this style see no. 21. Another artist whose work included the Satsuma style was Makuzu Kōzan. His work is well represented in the collection, but without a piece in Satsuma style, such as he had only made early in his career.

The porcelain of the Meiji period was more adventurous. We do not discuss here the large-scale porcelain manufacturers that grew up from the Imari tradition in Arita, and in more westernizing styles in or near Seto. The most famous of the former were the Fukugawa Seiji and the Koransha, while the most celebrated of the latter was to become the Noritake factory. A few individual potters, with private workshops varying from a few employees to those with some dozens, held closely to old traditions, making fine imitations of earlier wares. Suwa Sozan (no. 16) excelled in the imitation of classic Chinese porcelains, his modern work was less successful. Two potters stand out; Seifu Yohei and Makuzu Kōzan, the latter with a large and forward-looking factory, and with rapidly changing styles. Seifu was the more conservative of the two, less showy and colourful, but with elegance that greatly appealed to Japanese taste of the time. It is interesting that Seifu won more prizes in the competitive Domestic Expositions, while Kōzan won more International prizes. Miyagawa (Makuzu) Kōzan set up his factory in Yokohama shortly after 1870, when the port, as one of the few treaty ports, was full of foreigners. His first wares made there were exaggerated versions of a vaguely Satsuma-like style with high-relief animals and birds attached to vases and so-on. The contemporary critic Frank Brinkley described them as; 'specimens that disgrace the period of their manufacture': this was soon to change under two influences. Firstly, Kōzan sought the advice of Gottfried Wagener, an *oyatoi gaijin*, scientific polymath, who developed with Kōzan some new underglaze colours for porcelain, and secondly, it seems to have been the innovative approach of his adopted son Hanzan to whom he turned over the running of the factory in the 1880s, that ensured their success. The collection contains a good enough selection of the factory's work for the visitor or reader to see the wide range of its products and to note its high standards of quality (See nos. 4-13). When Kōzan died in 1916, Hanzan took the name Kōzan II, and began to work with stoneware as well as porcelain (See no.11). The factory was destroyed in World War II.

During the Meiji period metal-work developed in several ways; the carvers now made jars and flower-vases (no. 24), the casters also made relief-decorated vases (no. 31), and the incisers developed new skills in the imitation of brush-work fluency of line (see the remarkable fan by Unnō Shōmin, no. 28) but perhaps the most extraordinary new skill was the tinting of metals, the fusion of alloys, to produce a polychrome effect in metal (see the small metal plaque by Kajima Ikkoku II set in a lacquer box, no. 29).

The fastest developing of the crafts was probably cloisonné enamel. This was not an old craft in Japan, and probably no three-dimensional objects were made in cloisonné in Japan until the 1830s. It was then imitated from the Chinese by an amateur, Kaji Tsunekichi, from whom the industry, at first settled in Nagoya, was to spring. The development was one of better colours and skilful use of *cloisons*, the wire that was used to separate the colours. By the 1870s, larger areas could be made without the wire to prevent the colours running off during the innumerable firings necessary (see no. 34). This in turn allowed a change in style and pieces could be made that were not mostly pattern-making, but pictorial. From here the industry divided into two; the cheap mass-produced stuff for the lower end of the market, and the artist-craftsman-made pieces for the upper end of the market, for connoisseurs and for expositions. It is with this latter that we concern ourselves here. Again there was a division into two tendencies, that of the makers who attempted to imitate brush-paintings, exemplified by the work of Namikawa Sōsuke (no. 47) of Nagoya and then of Tōkyō, and those who unashamedly exploited the possibilities offered by the wire, exemplified by Namikawa Yasuyuki (no relation to Sōsuke) of Kyōto. The six pieces by Yasuyuki illustrated in this volume demonstrate the increasing skill of the artist and the way he developed his techniques, allowing changes in style and image (nos. 33–38).

Further developments of the craft included raised cloisonné, *moriage*, which sounds like a contradiction in terms (see no. 40 by Andō Jūbei, and for the apogee, no. 41 by Kumeno Teitarō) and so-called bodiless cloisonné, *plique-à-jour* (see no. 43), the latter imitated from

French craftsmen, notably Fernand Thesmar, whose work had been seen by Japanese cloisonné artists in Paris in 1900. By 1918 the market for expensive cloisonné had collapsed; thus the industry was only producing the best work for about forty years.

In contrast, lacquer work seems at first look to have been conservative, for there was no western industry with which to compete, but in fact, small innovations made a considerable difference to the finished product. Research was officially instigated, and copies of famous antique lacquers commissioned. Leading among the innovative lacquerers was Shibata Zeshin but there were others, too. A Lacquerers Society was set up in 1891 (was it a coincidence that this was the year that the Kiriu Kōshō Kaisha went bankrupt?) to draw together craftsmen from all over Japan. Tōkyō became the centre of the industry, to the detriment of Kyōto, but Kaga also remained a provincial centre. Again, there is a sharp division between the cheap and the expensive; the Ashmolean (at the time of going to press) owns no spectacular piece of Meiji lacquer, but has one or two fine pieces.

An offshoot was the style called Shibayama after the family of craftsmen of that name who may or may not have invented it. This demands minutely carved miniature bas-relief carvings of coral, ivory, pearl-shell or semi-precious stone to be set into a lacquer (or ivory) base, often in combination with other crafts such as cloisonné or silver filigree (see no. 50).

The carvers of Buddhistic statues were forced, by the abolition of Buddhism as the official State Religion, to adapt to other genres; many turned to wood or ivory carving of realistic western-style figures; this was encouraged by the government when they employed Vincenzo Ragusa, an Italian High Victorian-style sculptor as an *oyatoi gaijin*, an official teacher of western sculpture. Some of these carvers made wood sculptures of considerable size, others ivory figurines (*okimono*) and yet others, netsuke.

Meiji period Japan must have been an exciting place for the craftsman; cut-throat and competitive, no doubt, but always at the cutting-edge of innovation. We can see the results today in some of the finest and most skilled works of art-craft ever made.

The collection continues to grow; as we go to press the museum is attempting to purchase a superb *shibuichi* figure of a hawk by Jōmi Eisuke (1839–1899), a sculpture of purely Japanese inspiration, to form a comparison with the westernizing work of the mother and child bronze by Udagawa Kazuo (no. 32)

1 Needlework relief-decorated screen

The four classes
Two seals
1893
H. 182.0 cm; W. 276.0 cm; W. 18.2 cm; H. 69.0 cm
(each panel) Story Fund 1995.87

A four-fold screen, each panel applied in relief with silk figures depicting the Four Classes of Edo Japan. The reverse with a painting on silk of crows. Signed with two seals; illegible and ? *Setsugan*, and bearing the date 1st month 1893.

The technique of *oshi-e* is one of padded silk relief; silk wadding is covered with dyed and painted silk, adhering to the background paper. The fineness of detail is remarkable, and this screen would have been an extremely expensive item, particularly as the hard-wood-veneered frame is mounted in elaborate and very heavy soft-metal mounts, probably supplied by a former sword-fittings maker. The very heaviness of the screen as it is precludes the possibility of its sale to a Japanese buyer unless he lived in a European-style house. Its sheer quality suggests that it was made for one of the major International Expositions of the end of the nineteenth century; indeed the date 1893 found on a paper at the waist of a figure in the second uppermost register of the left-hand screen (the figure pulling a handcart) suggests that this would have been the World's Columbian Exposition in Chicago of that year. Our inability to read the uppermost seal, and our doubtful reading of the lower seal (? Setsugan) makes it impossible (so far) to find any record of the screen in that exhibition.

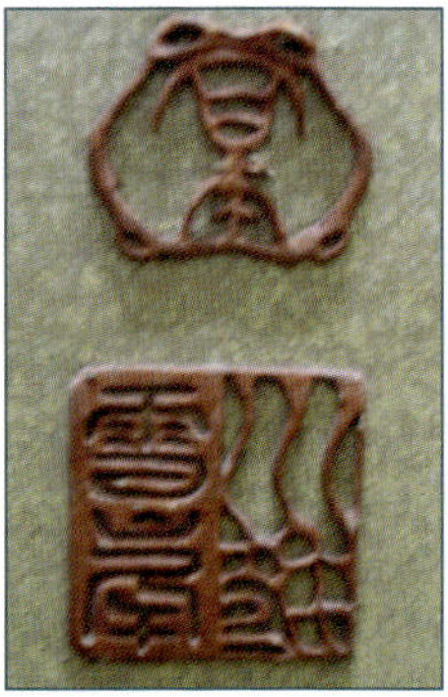

The subject-matter is the somewhat outdated one of the Four Classes of Edo period Japan; these had, of course, been abolished at the beginning of the Meiji period in 1868. Nevertheless, they are here represented one for each panel. Screens read from right to left, so the right hand panel represents the samurai and the warrior class. The second fold represents the farmer, here entirely

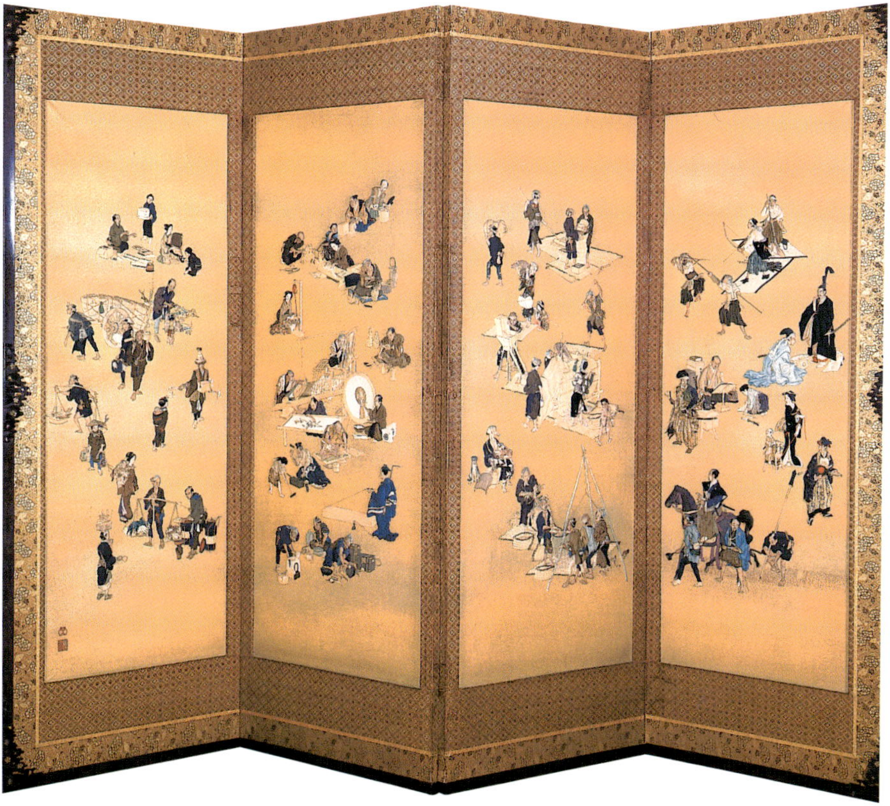

occupied in the production of rice. The third fold depicts the craftsmen; hat-makers, wood-turners, a woman fan-maker, a basket-maker, a woman braid-maker, a sculptor, weavers, an embroiderer, an umbrella-maker and a potter, sword-smiths, a carpenter and bronze-casters. The left-hand panel depicts the merchant class, the lowest class in society.

2 Embroidered silk hanging

Cranes, cycads and wisteria
Unsigned
c. 1905
H. 201.0 cm; W. 279.0 cm

Gift of Sir Herbert Ingram 1958.81

Large silk hanging embroidered in coloured silks, within a silk and metal thread brocade border. The whole backed with a cotton *tsutsugaki* fabric. The design is of five Japanese Cranes (*Grus japonica;* Japanese *tanchō*) standing on rocks and grass amid cycads and white wisteria. The added border has a repeating dragon motif and the reverse, stylised chrysanthemum flowers. The four panels were carefully designed to compose one large piece, not a four-fold screen, by the careful placing of the extra-long inflorescences of the wisteria along the joins.

The ground fabric is a black, finely ribbed silk. The embroidery is mainly satin stitch, couching stitching and knotwork. The range of textures is achieved through the use of threads of various thicknesses and varying degrees of twist. The glossy feathers, for example, are stitched with floss silk of practically no twist, whereas the rougher bark and rocks are worked in a combination of loosely and tightly twisted threads. Clusters of knots create moss and lichen texture on the rocks. The direction of the stitches reflects the natural growth patterns of feathers and the scaly nature of the cranes' legs and feet. The effect of the water surface in the lower right of the embroidery is achieved by individually couching down the long and extremely fine silk threads and incorporating slightly thicker threads to form the pattern of ripples.

It is impossible to identify this magnificent and high-quality panel with any entry in Ingram's somewhat perfunctory diary, or his list of purchases made in 1908. This is surprising as it would have been extremely expensive; it may not have been bought on this trip.

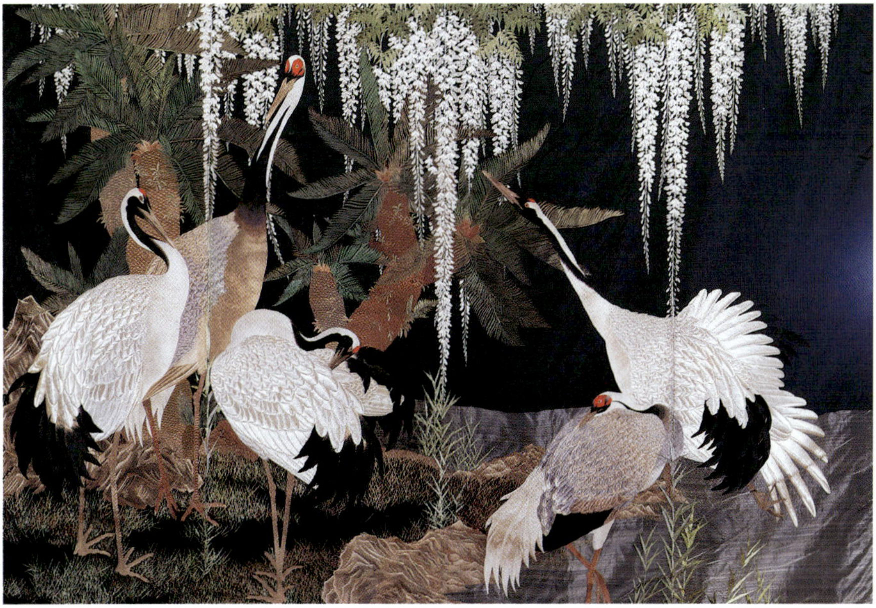

3 Embroidered screen

Cormorant-fishing
Signed
1900-1910
H. 169.3 cm; W. 267.0 cm — Story Fund 2000.3

A four-panel screen embroidered in silk in a lacquer and calamander-wood frame. The scene is of cormorant-fishing by night, with birds perched on a boat with burning braziers at either end. Inscribed on a copper plaque: *Iida & Co. 'Takashimaya' Kyōto, Tōkyō, Yokohama.*

The composition of the screen follows the left hand of a pair of screens by Takeuchi Seihō (1864–1942), now in the Ōshajō Museum, Hiroshima (Ōshajō Bijutsu Hōmotsukan Shōzō). Seihō had spent some time in Gifu in the late nineties observing and sketching the cormorant-fishing, and some of the sketches, including some for the original of this screen, are in Kyōto City Art Museum. Seihō was an admirer of Turner and had read much of Ruskin's work; he visited Europe more than once and was present at the Paris Exposition of 1900.

Shinshichi Iida founded the Takashimaya Iida Company as a clothing store in Kyōto in 1831, and by 1909 it was a major store with several outlets in Japan. In 1930, the corporate name was changed to Takashimaya Co. Ltd, the name it retains today. Seihō acted as chief designer for textiles, including cut-velvet and needlework, though the company also used other artists. The lacquered wooden frame and lower panels are closely similar to a screen by the same company exhibited at the Japan-British Exposition at Shepherd's Bush in London in 1910 (Cat. No. 237) depicting flowers in the style of Sōtatsu. The company exhibited a screen 'with a dark ground' at Liège in 1906, but we do not know the subject-matter. Might it have been this?

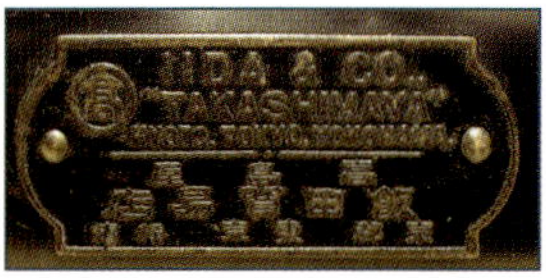

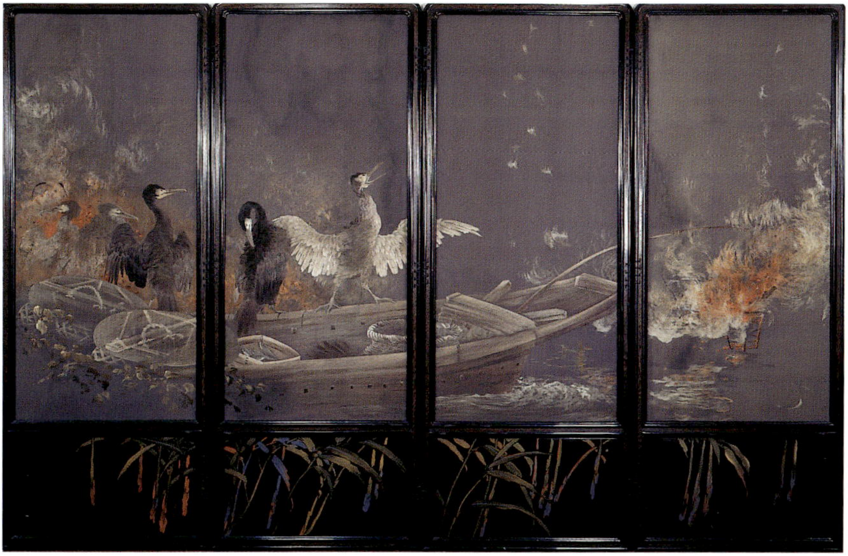

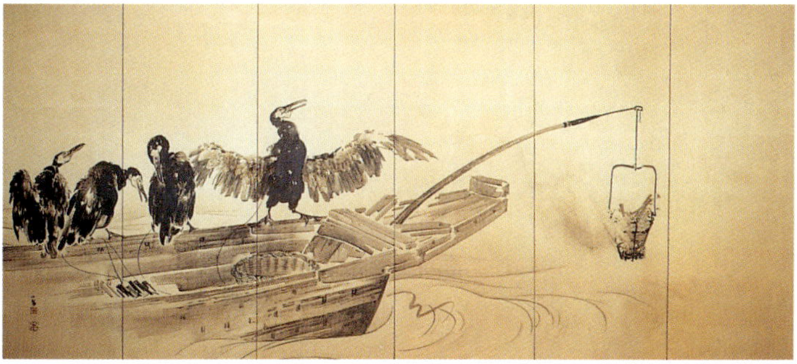

Screen by Takeuchi Seihō

4 Porcelain Vase

Moulded body, with underglaze red
By Makuzu Kōzan
Signed
1890s
H. 23.6 cm Story Fund 1996.132

Squat baluster porcelain vase with moulded white body and three panels painted in underglaze copper red with chickens, temple buildings in a landscape with Mount Fuji and samurai with attendants beside a stream. Silver mounted rim. Signed with underglaze blue seal-mark on the base; *Makuzu gama Kōzan sei* (*made at the Makuzu Kōzan kiln*).

The deeply moulded pattern resembles that on a vase, now in the Khalili Collection, that Miyagawa (Makuzu) Kōzan (1842–1916) exhibited at the World's Columbian Exposition in Chicago in 1893. His family name was Miyagawa, but he is usually referred to by his art name, Makuzu. His kiln was at Ōta, in Yokohama, and such was his versatility that he was sometimes, in his lifetime, called 'The wizard of Ōta'. Kōzan was so eclectic in his choice of styles that it is difficult to date his work; the most successful dating system is based upon the shape and style of the signature, for he seems to have changed the signature several times. The blue and white seal-style signatures are actually written, not stamped.

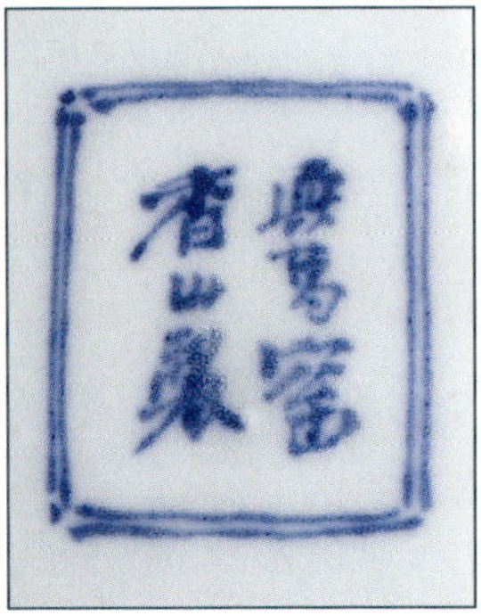

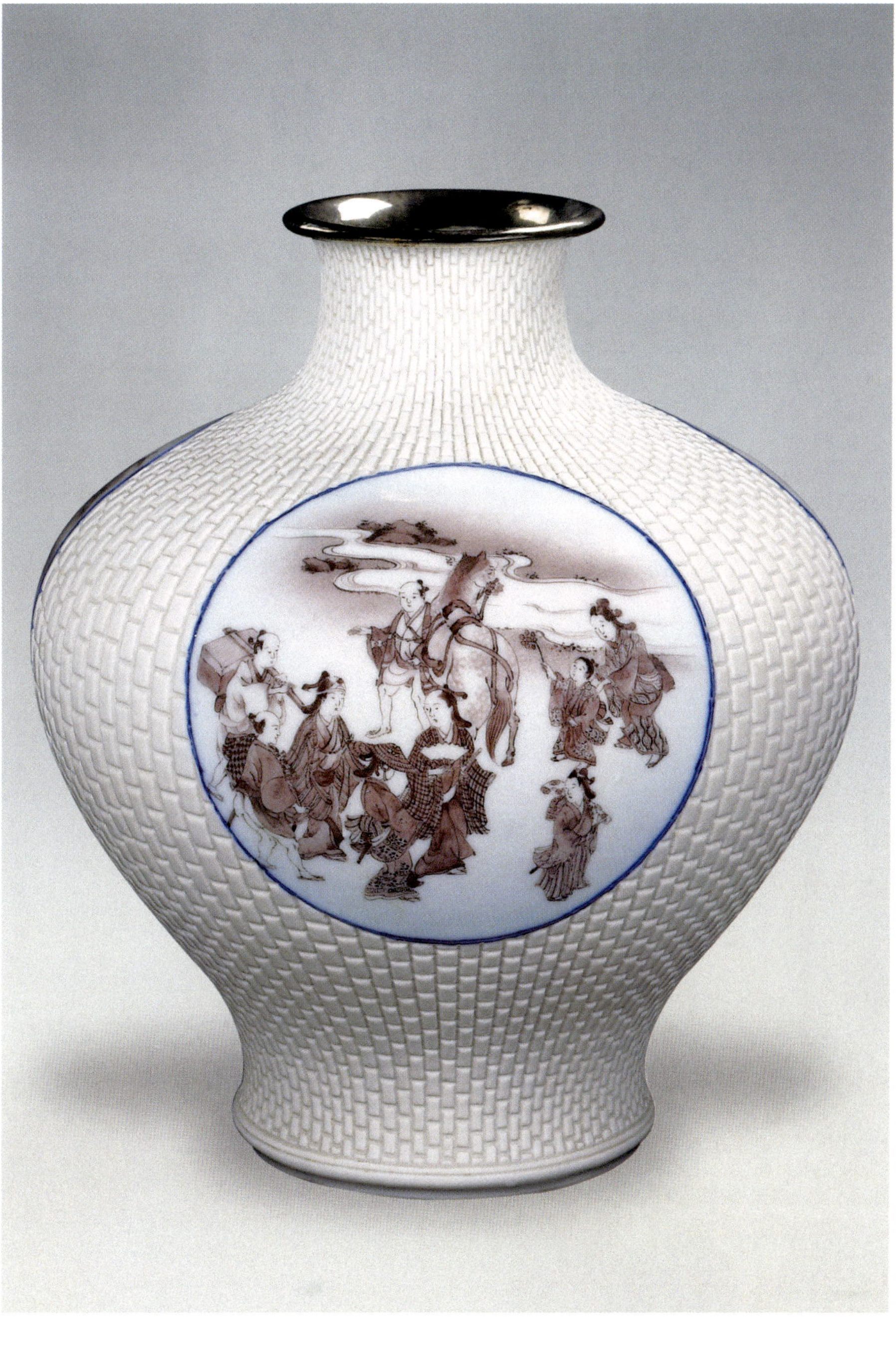

5 Porcelain vase

Moulded with chrysanthemums in a yellow glaze
By Miyagawa Hanzan
(Makuzu Kōzan factory)
Signed
c. 1895
H. 35.0 cm — Story Fund 1996.55

Baluster shaped porcelain vase decorated with a yellow glaze over chrysanthemum heads in low relief. Signed on base in underglaze blue: *Makuzu gama Hanzan sei.*

Miyagawa Hanzan (Hannosuke, 1859–1940) was Kōzan's nephew and adopted son. Kōzan handed over the running of the kiln to Hanzan in 1890, though the name remained unchanged, and most pieces were made bearing the 'signature' of Kōzan; pieces like this, signed Hanzan are very uncommon and we do not know why they exist at all. Hanzan took the name Kōzan II on the death of his adopted father in 1916.

All the prizes that the factory continued to win in both International and National Expositions were awarded in the name Makuzu (Miyagawa) Kōzan. In 1896, Kōzan I was named an Artist of the Imperial Court (*Teishitsu gigei in*).

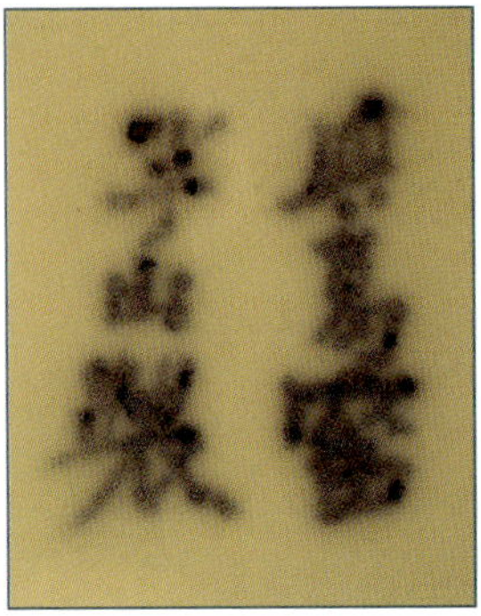

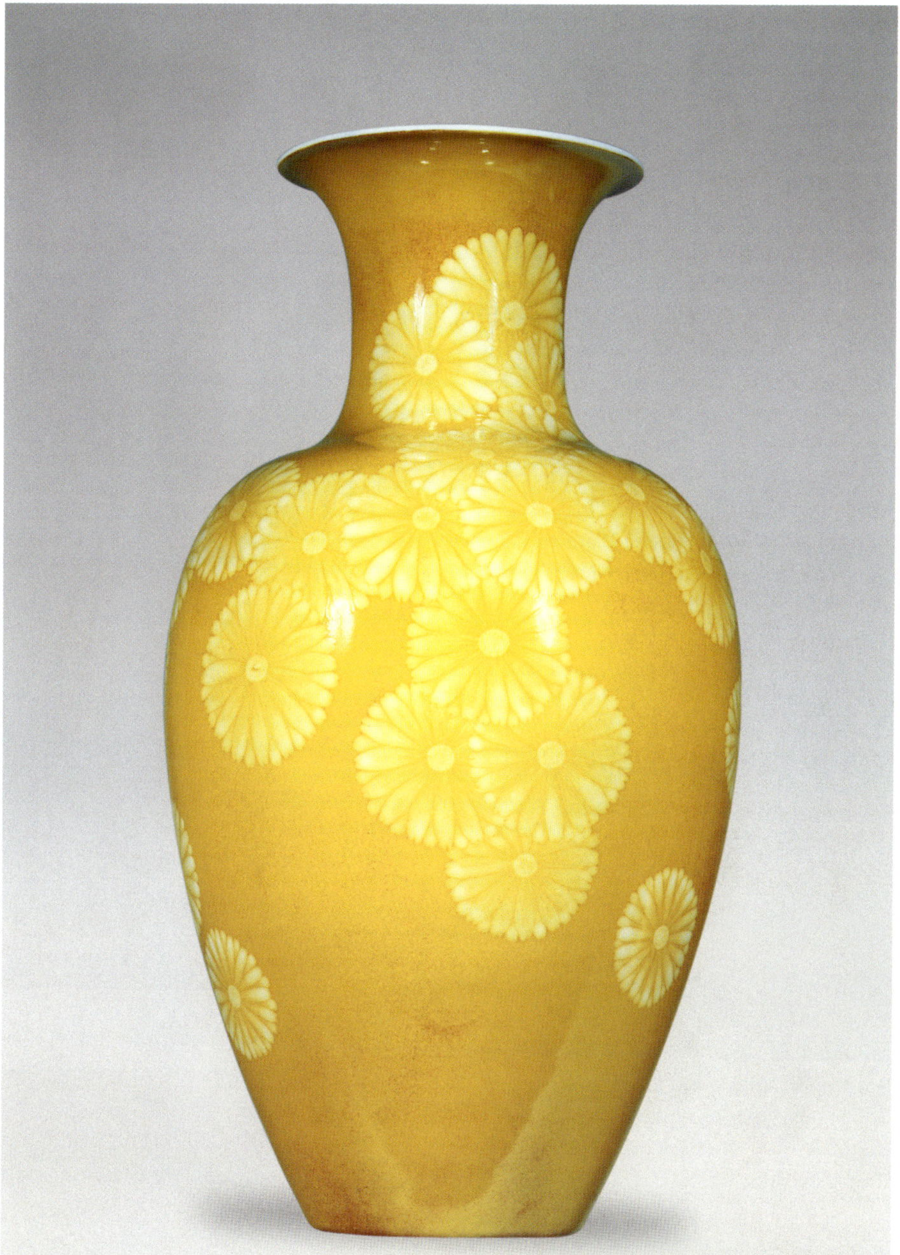

6 Porcelain vase

Underglaze red and peach-bloom
By Makuzu Kōzan
Signed
c. 1895
H. 12.4 cm Gift of Sir Herbert Ingram 1956.667

Small baluster-shaped vase with wide neck and slightly everted rim. Decorated under a pale uneven peach-bloom glaze with a procession of three insects holding various flowers. Seal-mark in underglaze blue on the base: *Makuzu Kōzan sei.*

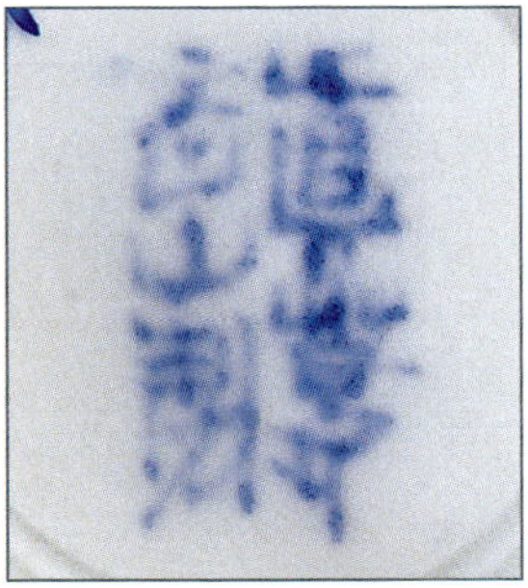

Kōzan made several shapes and sizes of vases with a peach-bloom glaze decorated with underglaze copper-red drawings of processions of insects carrying flowers as if they were banners. These, cariacatures of Edo period *daimyō* processions, derive from paintings by artists such as Nishiyama Hōen (1804–1867), themselves possibly inspired by the twelfth century *Chōjō giga* handscrolls. Bought in Japan by Sir Herbert and Lady Ingram in 1908.

7 & 8 Two porcelain vases

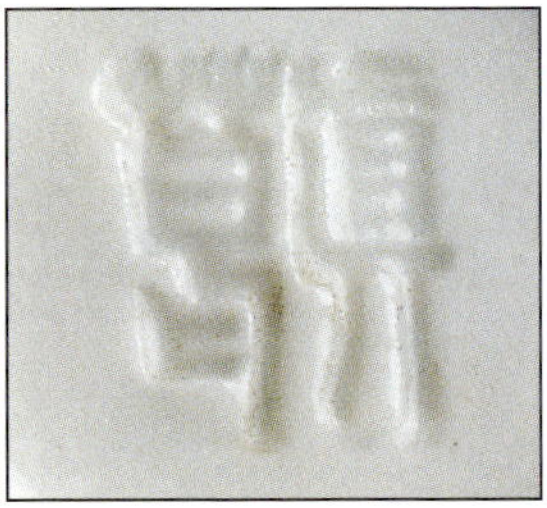

Peach-bloom
By Makuzu Kōzan
Sealed
c. 1895
H. 6.3 cm and 5.7 cm
Gift of Sir Herbert Ingram 1956.682 & 1956.1853

Small baluster-shaped vase with flattened shoulders and rounded rim, covered in an uneven peach-bloom glaze. Impressed seal on base: *Makuzu.*

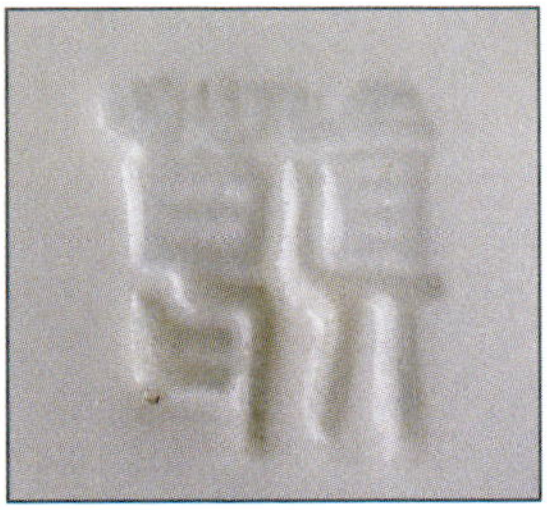

Small bulbous vase with sharply angled sides and rounded rim, covered in an uneven peach-bloom glaze. Impressed seal on base: *Makuzu.*

So good was Kōzan's imitation of Chinese monochrome glazes that he was accused of forgery. It was not Kōzan who was the forger, but the dealers who sold to foreign clients who could not read the impressed seal marks.

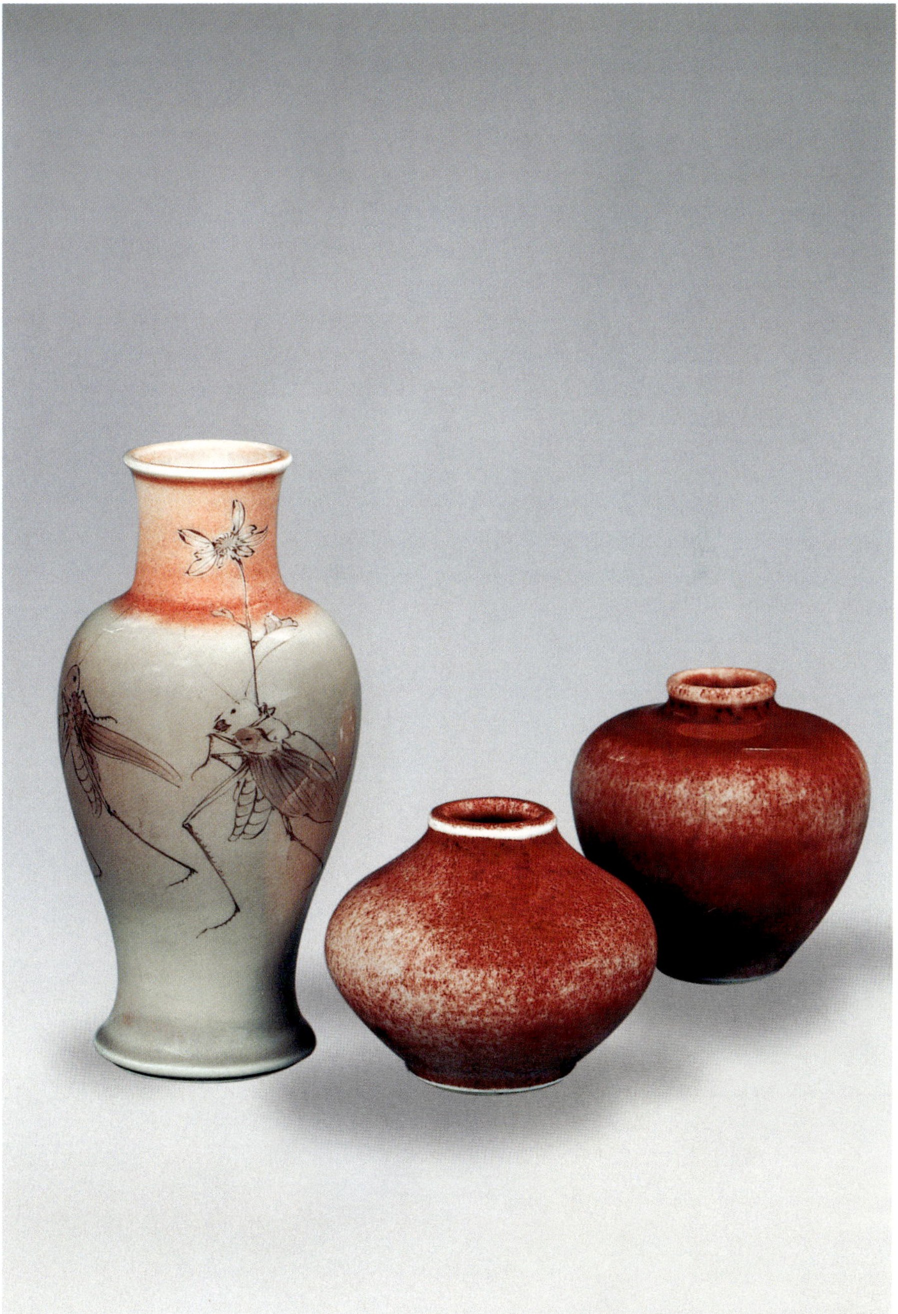

9 Porcelain vase

White, pink and mauve flowers on a green ground
By Makuzu Kōzan
Signed
c. 1900-1910
H. 32.0 cm — Story Fund 1991.1

Baluster-shaped porcelain vase decorated in underglaze green, white and mauve with raised white enamel, showing clumps of flowers on a mottled green ground. Signed on base in underglaze blue: *Makuzu Kōzan sei*.

New underglaze colours, such as pink and green, colours that would stand a high temperature firing, were developed around this time, partly through the assistance of Gottfried Wagener, a scientific polymath, who was an *oyotoi gaijin*, a foreigner employed by the Japanese government to develop Japanese industry and art industry. Kōzan was one of the first to seek his advice, and to exploit the full range of these colours (as was Namikawa Yasuyuki for enamel; see nos. 33–38).

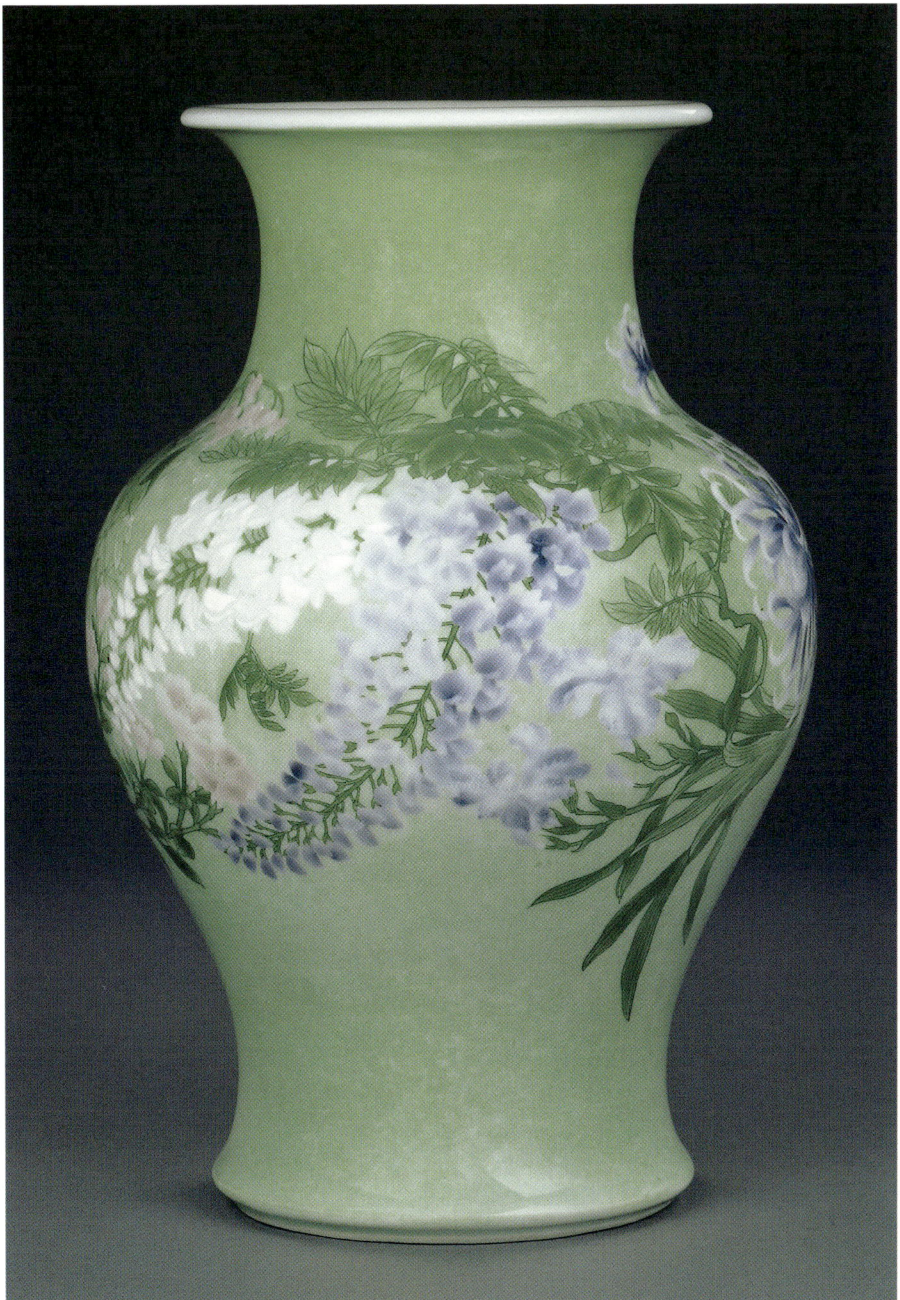

10 Large porcelain vase

Blue and white
Trees
By Makuzu Kōzan
Signed
c. 1910
H. 86.0 cm — Story Fund 2000.47

Very large porcelain vase decorated in underglaze blue with tall trees and bamboo in winter. Signed in underglaze blue on base: *Makuzu Kōzan sei.*

Kōzan was making very large vases from the 1890s onwards. At Chicago in 1893 he had exhibited an enormous stoneware vase; the porcelain vases of this sort of size appear to date from about 1910–1915.

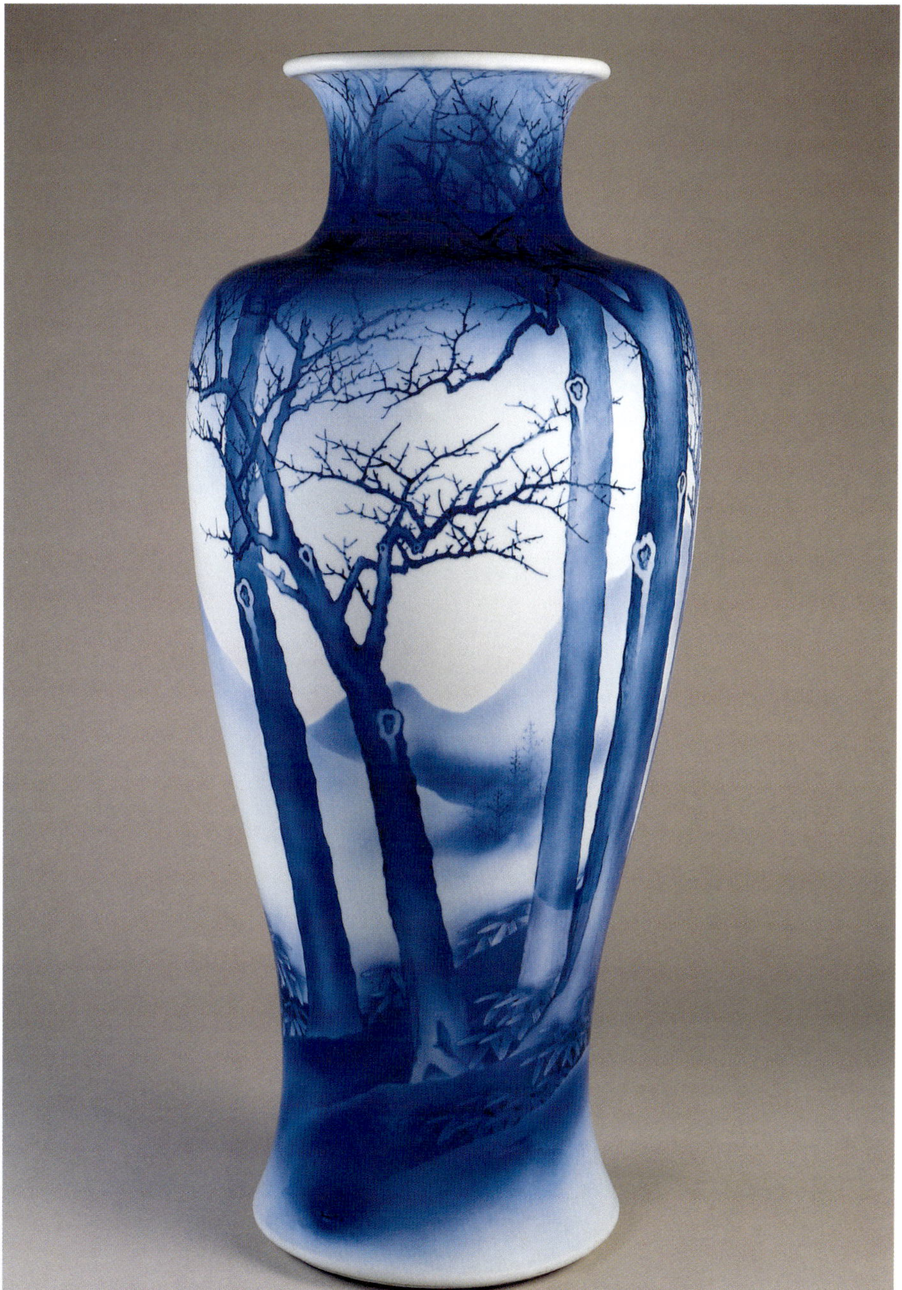

11 Stoneware vase

Celadon with modelled shrimp
By Makuzu Kōzan
Sealed
1915 or later
H.26.0 cm

Story Fund 1990.1

Globular stoneware vase partially glazed in pale green, leaving much of the rough body unglazed, with engraved decoration on the neck and body, with a prawn modelled in high relief on the body. Impressed seal on base: Hanzan in a double gourd.

Shortly before Kōzan I's death in 1916, the factory began to make stoneware vessels in the manner of the Iga kilns, admittedly somewhat remotely, even using the local Shigaraki clay and glazes; most of these are based on old Japanese shapes, usually related to the tea ceremony - this might have been a *mizusashi*, though the box does not say so.

The original box (lost before the pot reached the museum), was inscribed with the character for Iga (Christie's, London, 7 March, 1989, lot 453).

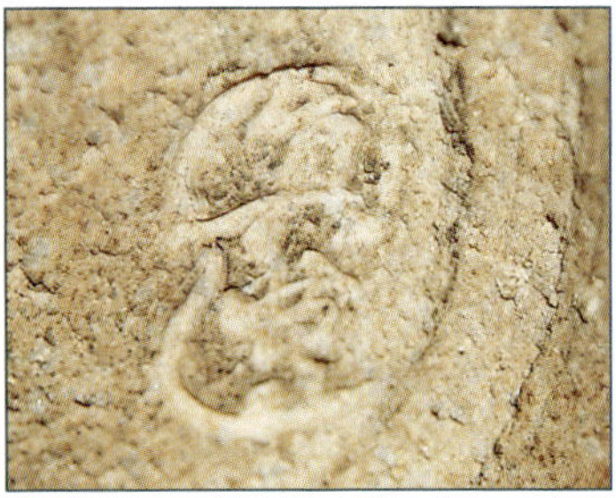

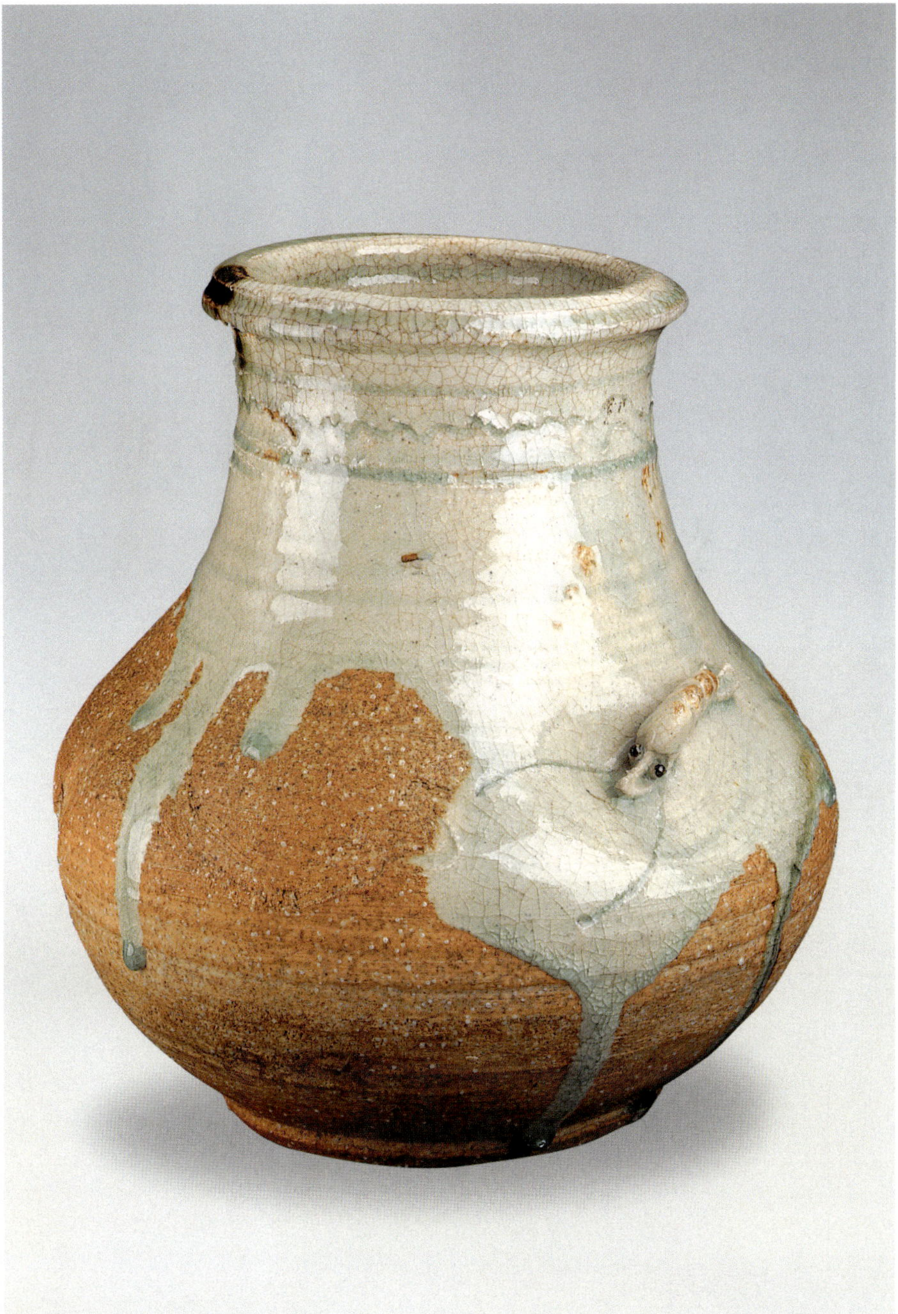

12 Earthenware bowl

By Miyagawa Kōzan II
Signed
c. 1925
D. 18.2 cm

Story Fund 2000.181

Pottery bowl, the edge partly waved and pierced, decorated with underglaze blue and brown and slip with a pine branch. The exterior similar. In the manner of Dōhachi. Signed: *Kōzan.*

After the death of Kōzan I, Hanzan, by then Kōzan II, went through a period of the making of wares for Japanese use, usually related to the tea ceremony, in the manner of Nin'ami Dōhachi (1783–1855), a remote follower of Nonomura Ninsei (*c.*1574–1660/6), using broad calligraphic style decoration on asymmetric shapes, and slip decoration.

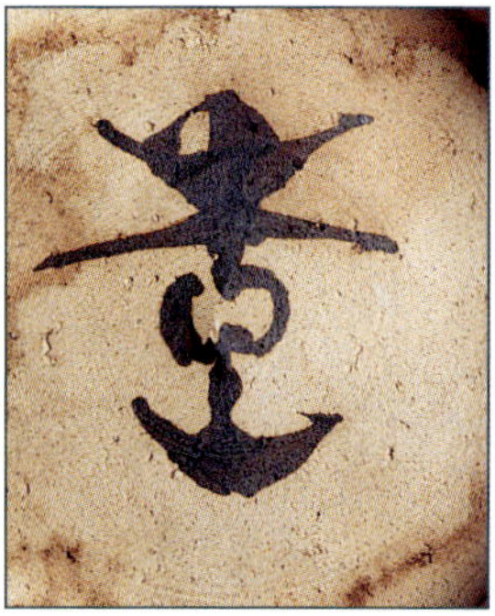

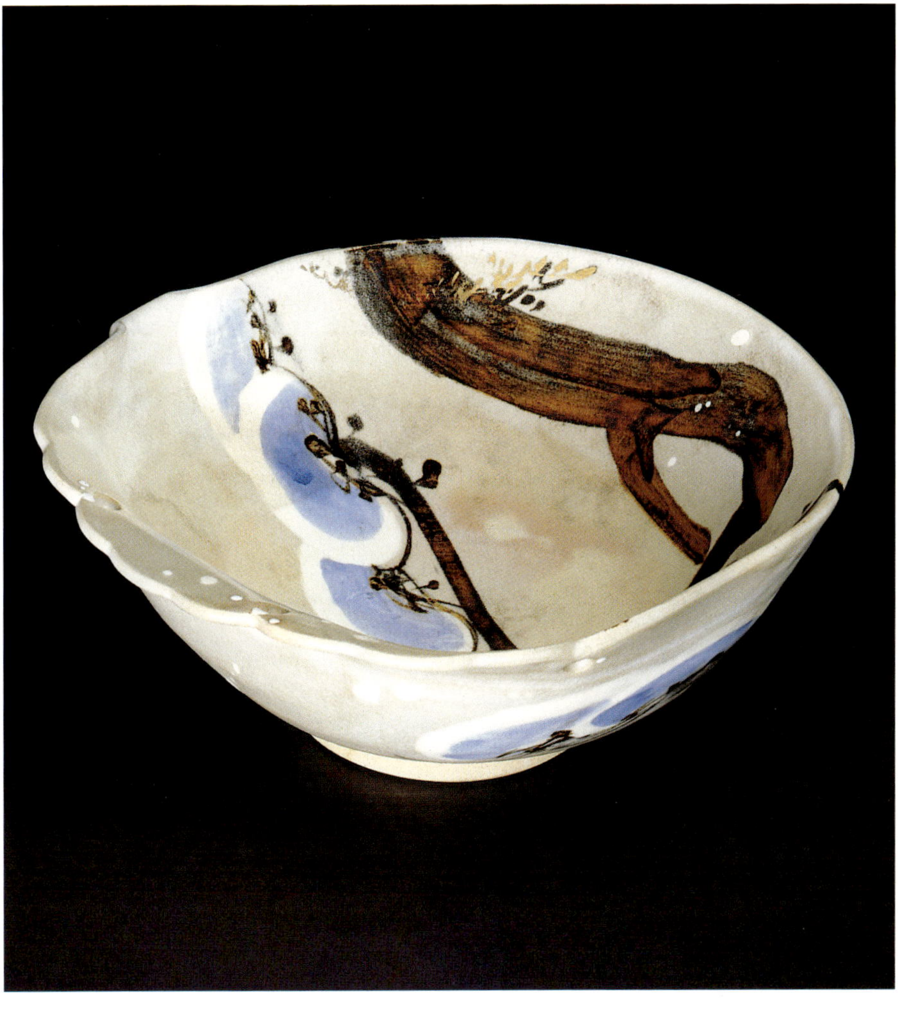

13 Porcelain bottle

Green flambé
Attributed to Makuzu Kōzan
Sealed
c. 1890s
H. 22.5 cm

Story Fund 1989.13

Pear-shaped porcelain bottle with flared neck covered in a green flambé glaze. Impressed gourd-shaped seal on base: *Kōji* (?) in a double gourd.

Kōzan was experimenting with flambé and transmutation glazes in the manner developed at Limoges and Copenhagen, some of which depended on Chinese originals, from the early 1880s. Flambé glazes intermingle colours seamlessly in an amazing variety. We are not sure of the date of this exquisite bottle, but believe it to be from the late nineteenth century.

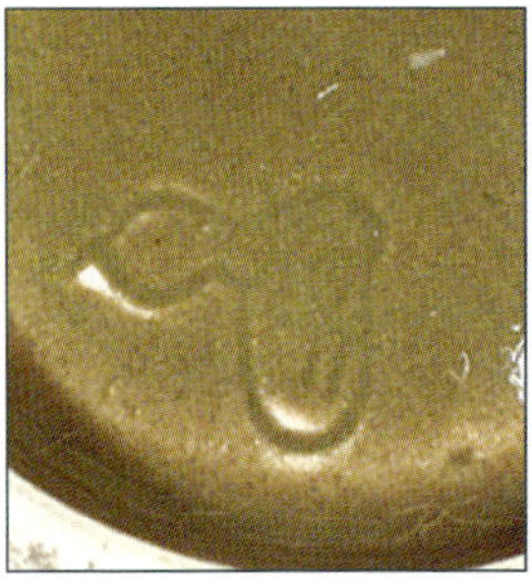

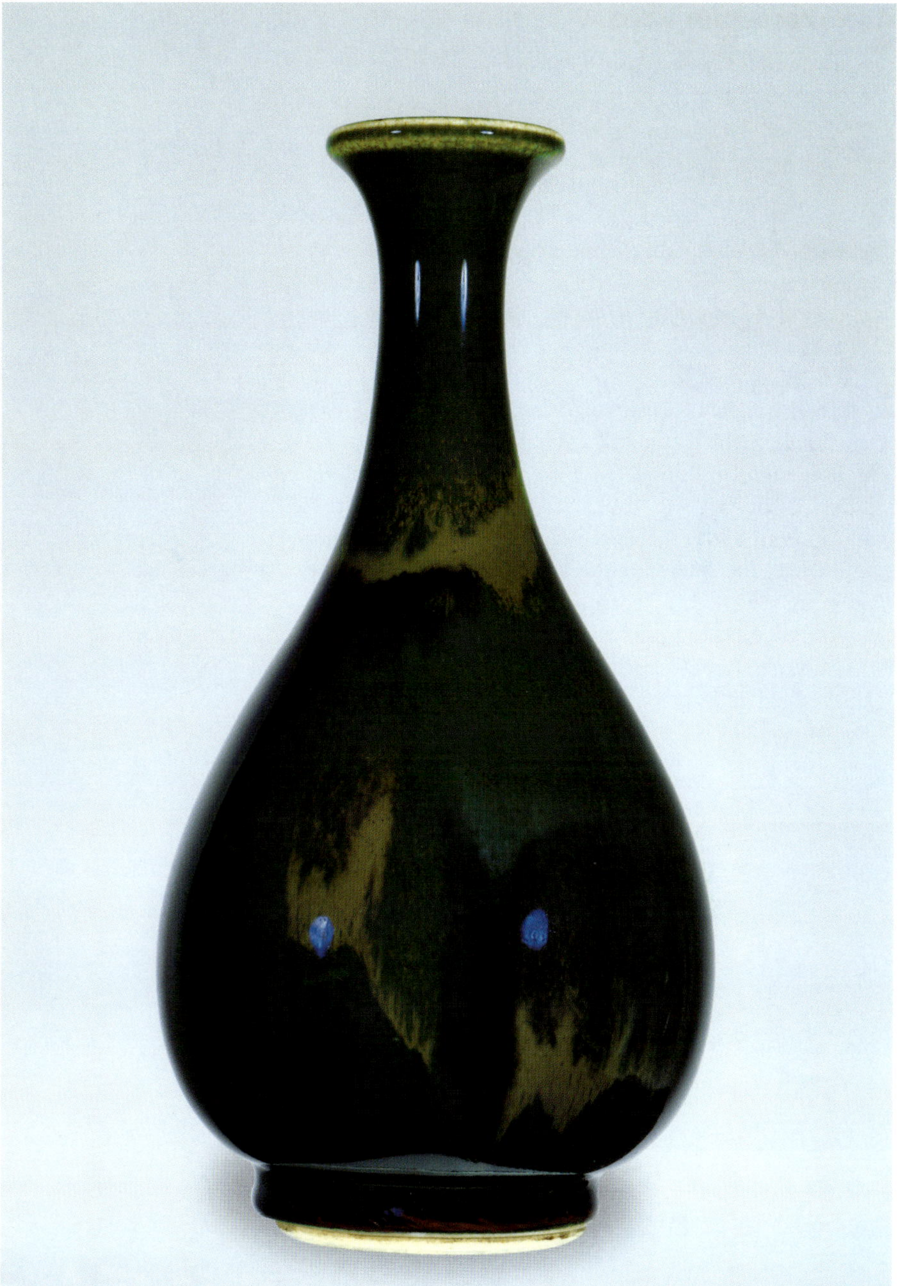

14 Porcelain vase

Moulded with an ivory glaze
By Seifū Yohei III
Signed
c. 1900
H. 28.7 cm — Gift of David King 1993.398

Porcelain vase of tapering shape with wide shoulders and indented mouth, decorated in low relief, self-coloured on an ivory ground, with narcissus and wagtail. Incised signature on base: *Dai Nihon Seifū zū (Great Japan made by Seifū.)*

Where Makuzu Kōzan won prizes at the International Expositions, Seifū Yohei (1851–1914) won more prizes at the domestic Expositions, a nice comment on subtle differences of taste; in the Fourth National Industrial Exposition in 1895, the extremely knowledgeable judges commented 'the shape [of the vase] is perfect... and his skill is unparalleled in Japan... He is a model for other potters'. He was the son of the Maruyama school painter Okada Ryōhei, studied painting under the *nanga* artist Tanomura Chokunyū (1814–1907), and then was adopted by Seifū II, becoming Seifū III in 1878.

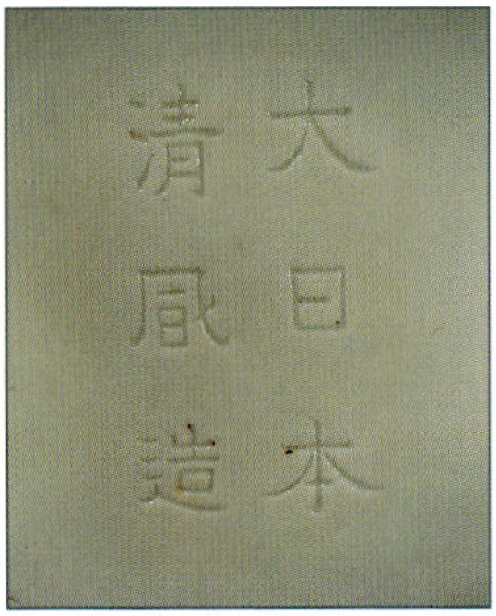

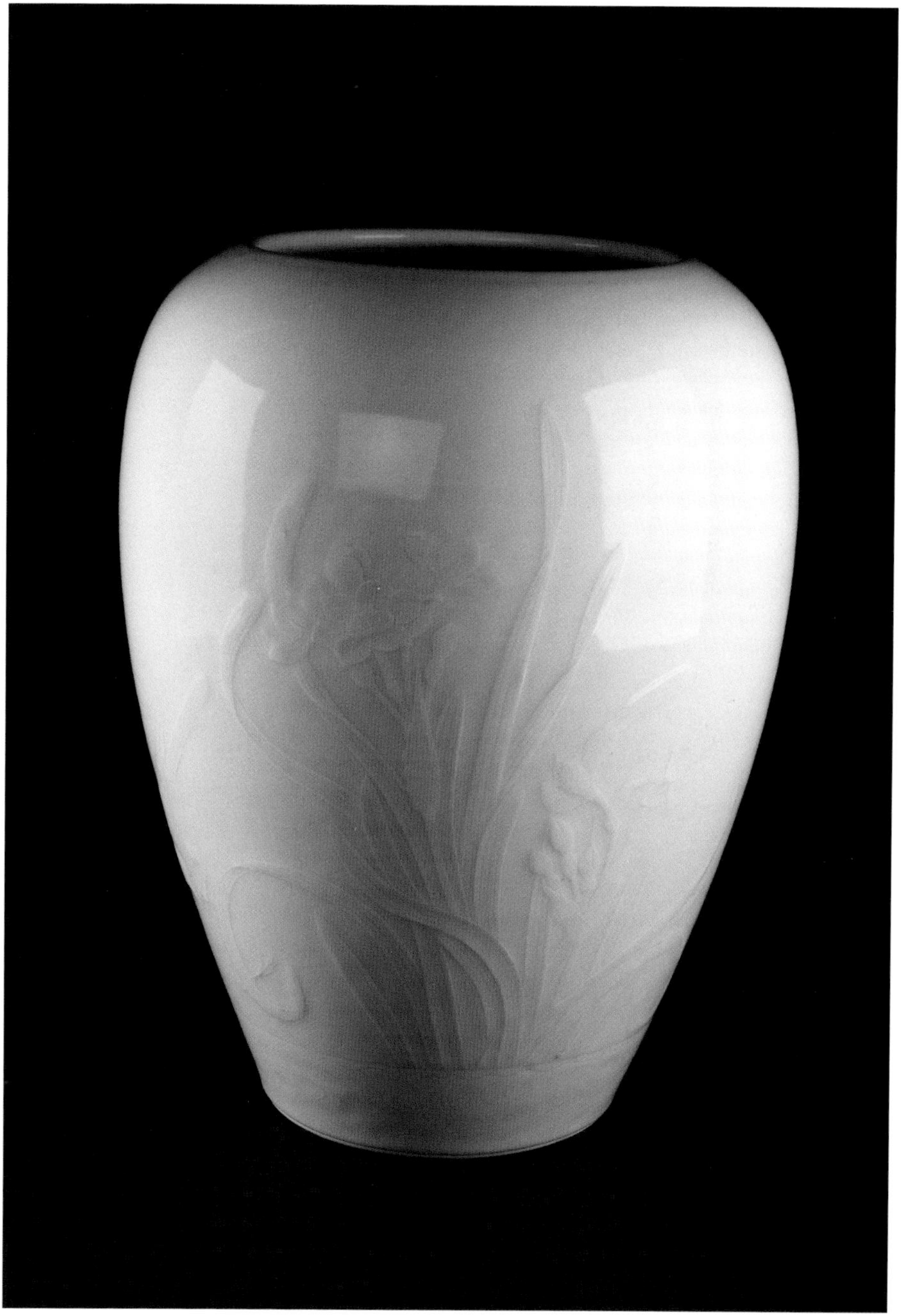

15 Moulded vase

Underglaze blue, and pink and white glazes
Cranes and pine
By Seifū Yohei III
Signature
c. 1910
H. 44.0 cm Story Fund 1993.399

Tall inverted baluster vase with low relief moulding of two cranes in colours on an underglaze blue pine tree, with a pink and white ground. Incised signature on base within two underglaze blue circles: *Dai Nihon Seifū zū.*

Seifū I had been a pupil of Nin'ami Dōhachi (see no.12) in Kyōto; the family kiln was set up in Gojōzaka. This is an unusually showy piece.

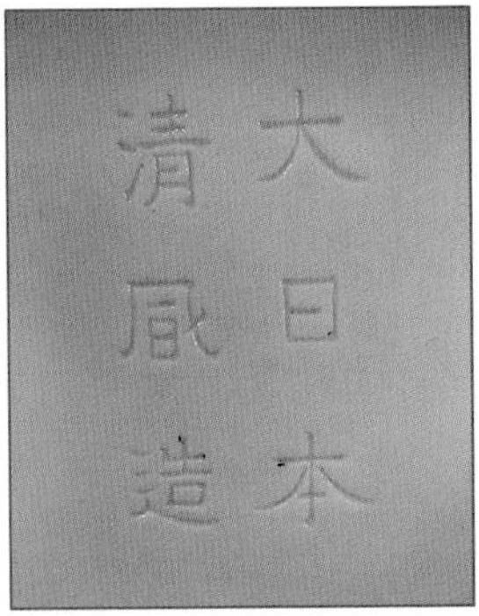

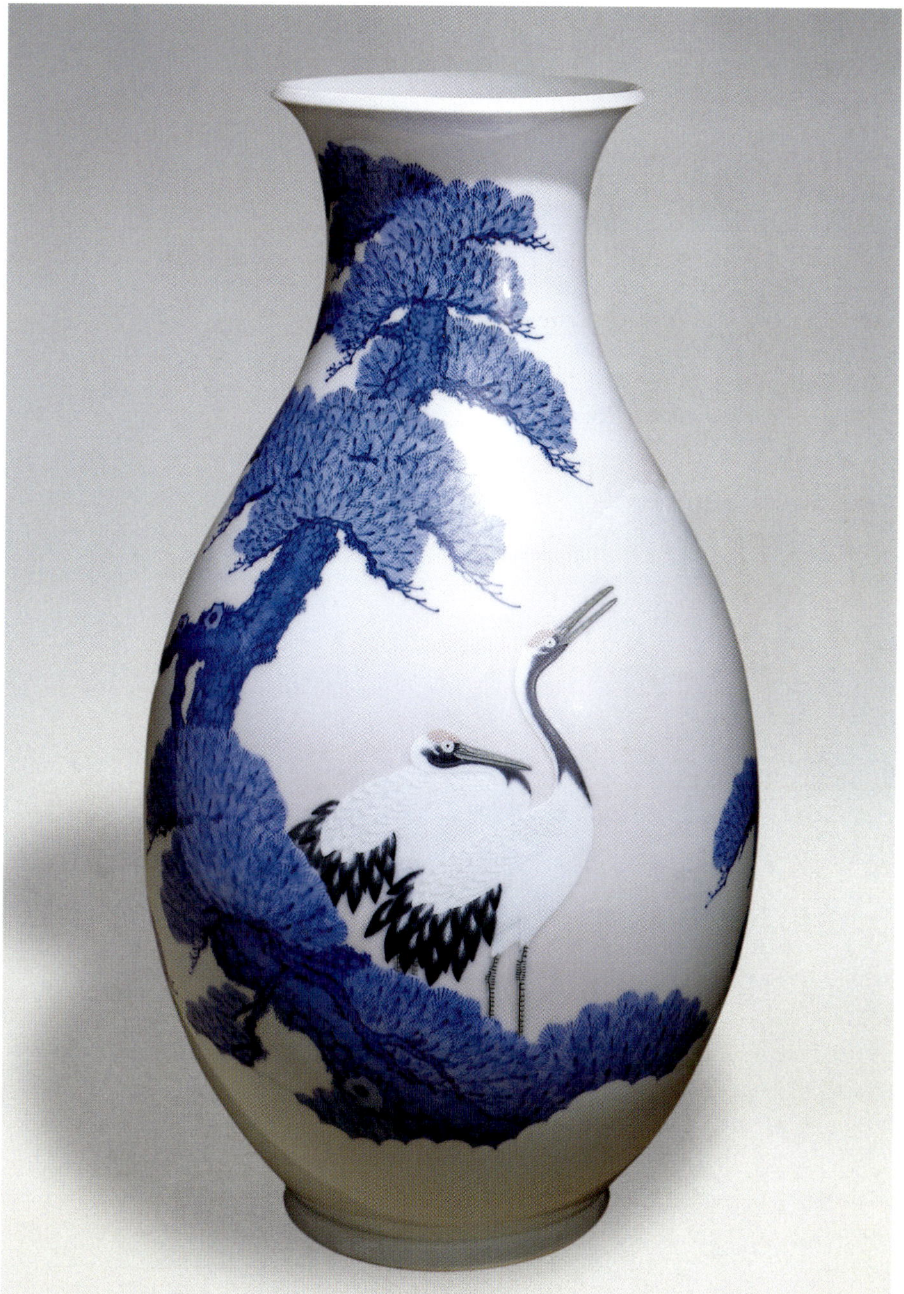

16 Porcelain vase

Celadon
By Suwa Sozan
Sealed
c. 1910
H. 30.0 cm

Story Fund 1995.68

Vase with ovoid body, tall thick neck strongly ribbed circumferentially with everted lip. Impressed round seal on base: *Sozan*.

Sozan specialized in the imitation of Chinese wares, particularly the celadon wares of the Song and Yuan dynasties. This is a direct copy of a Song original.

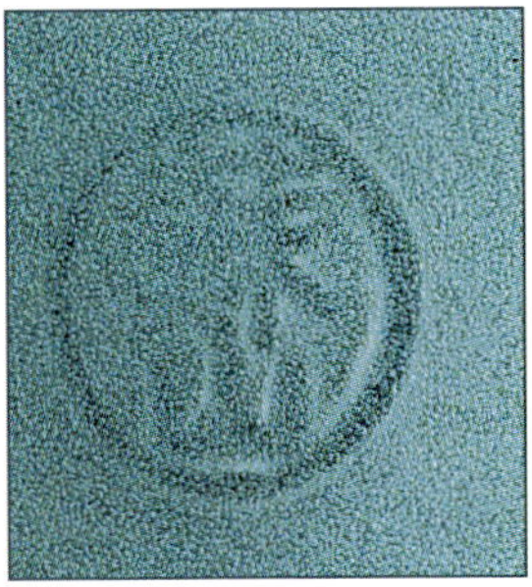

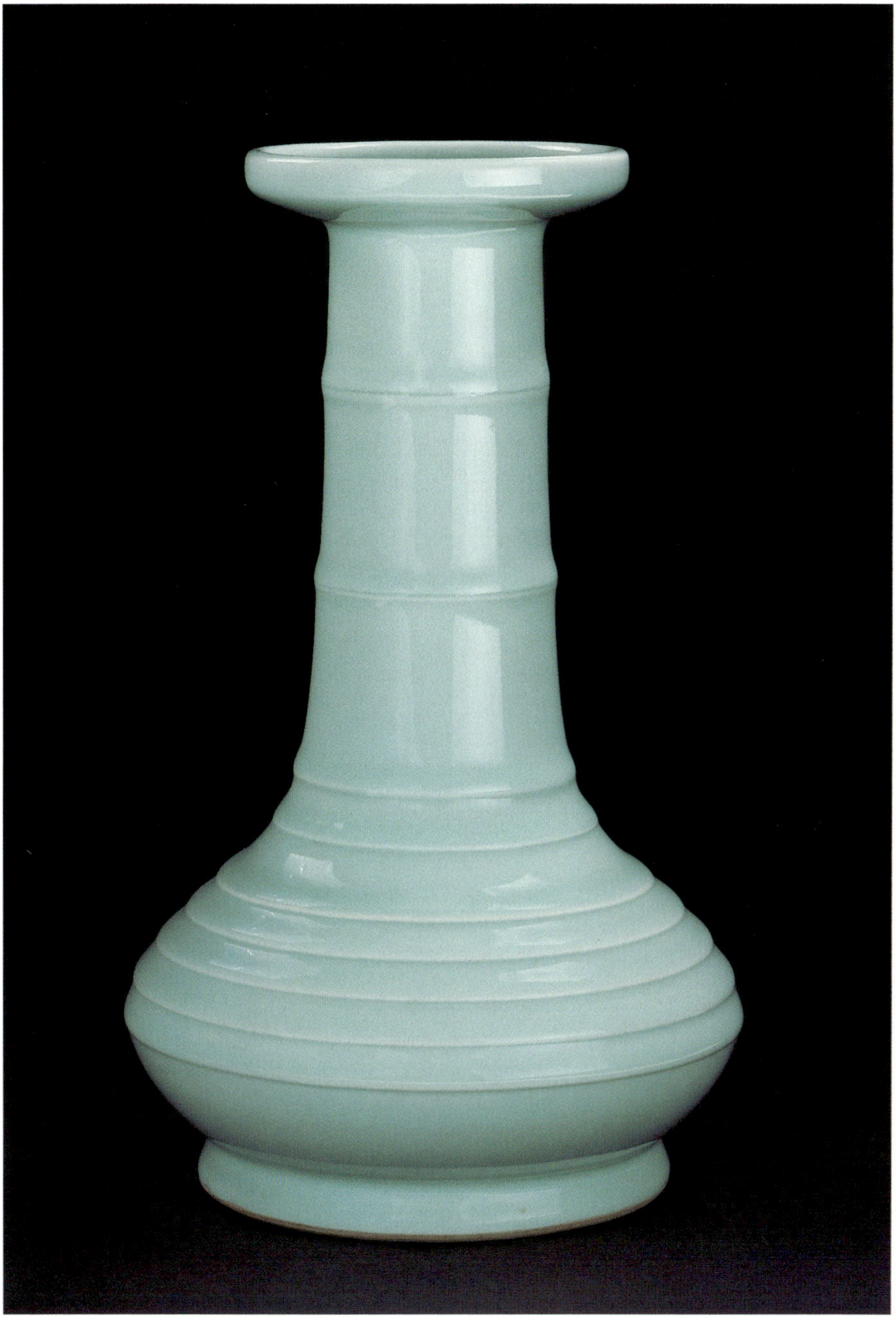

17 Porcelain vase

Overglaze enamels
Ship in a stormy sea
By Namikawa Sōsuke
Signed
early 1880s
H. 37.3 cm

Story Fund 1999.42

Porcelain vase with enamelled depiction of a ship in difficulties in a violent thunderstorm. Signed on base in iron red: *Dai Nihon Tōkyō Namikawa sei; Hōen ga (Great Japan Tōkyō, made by Namikawa; painted by Hōen)*.

Namikawa Sōsuke had moved the Shippō Kaisha factory from Nagoya to Tōkyō when he took it over in 1880, continuing to make cloisonné enamel, but he also seems to have had other factories, or at least acted as agent for other factories making cloisonné on a porcelain body and porcelain itself. Very few examples of porcelain signed by this factory (or these factories) have been identified. The painter is identified as Hōen (not Nishiyama Hōen), but is otherwise unknown.

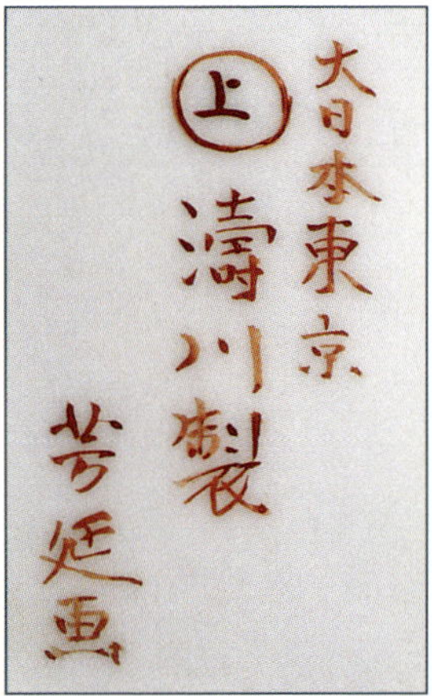

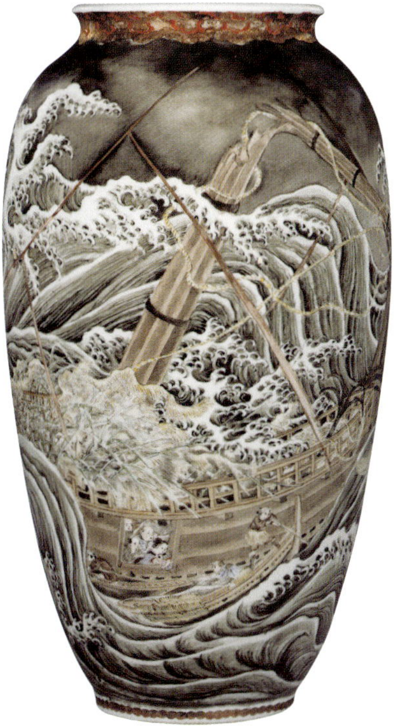

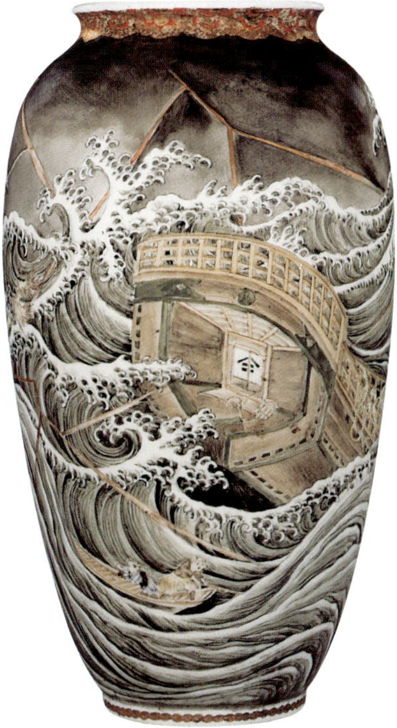

18 Earthenware dish

Overglaze enamels
Landscape
By Kinkōzan Sōbei VII
Signed
c. 1900
W. 36.7 cm

Story Fund 1992.71

Earthenware plate decorated with a landscape in westernized perspective, in detailed polychrome enamels with underglaze blue and gilding, within a lobed border. The image signed: *Itsuzan*. Signed under the base, a seal-mark in underglaze blue within a gold key fret border *Kinkōzan zō*. With an iron red seal: *Chokusai*. A further factory label in English.

The Kinkōzan factory was an old one, having made *Kyō-yaki* for several generations. The sixth generation master, modernised the Kyōto factory, specializing in high quality Satsuma-style decorated wares. His son, Sōbei VII (1868–1927), succeeded his father in 1884. In this fairly typical plate, of excellent quality, it is interesting to see how the painter (presumably Itsuzan) has not quite understood European geometric perspective, for though there is recession vertically, there is no fixed viewpoint, and the eye is always at a right-angle to the horizontal area, just as if viewing a Japanese screen.

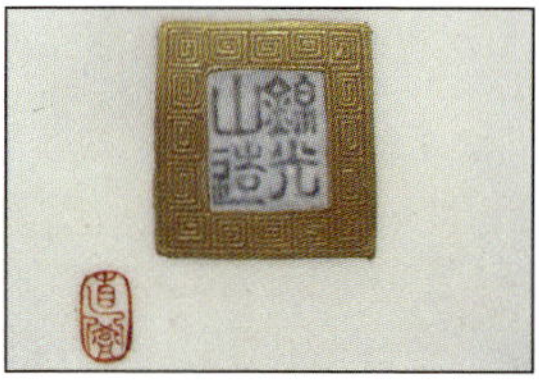

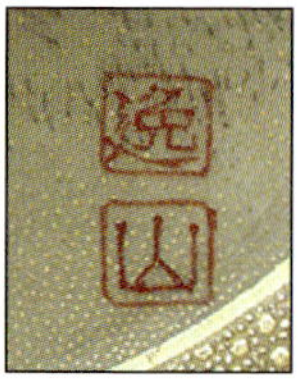

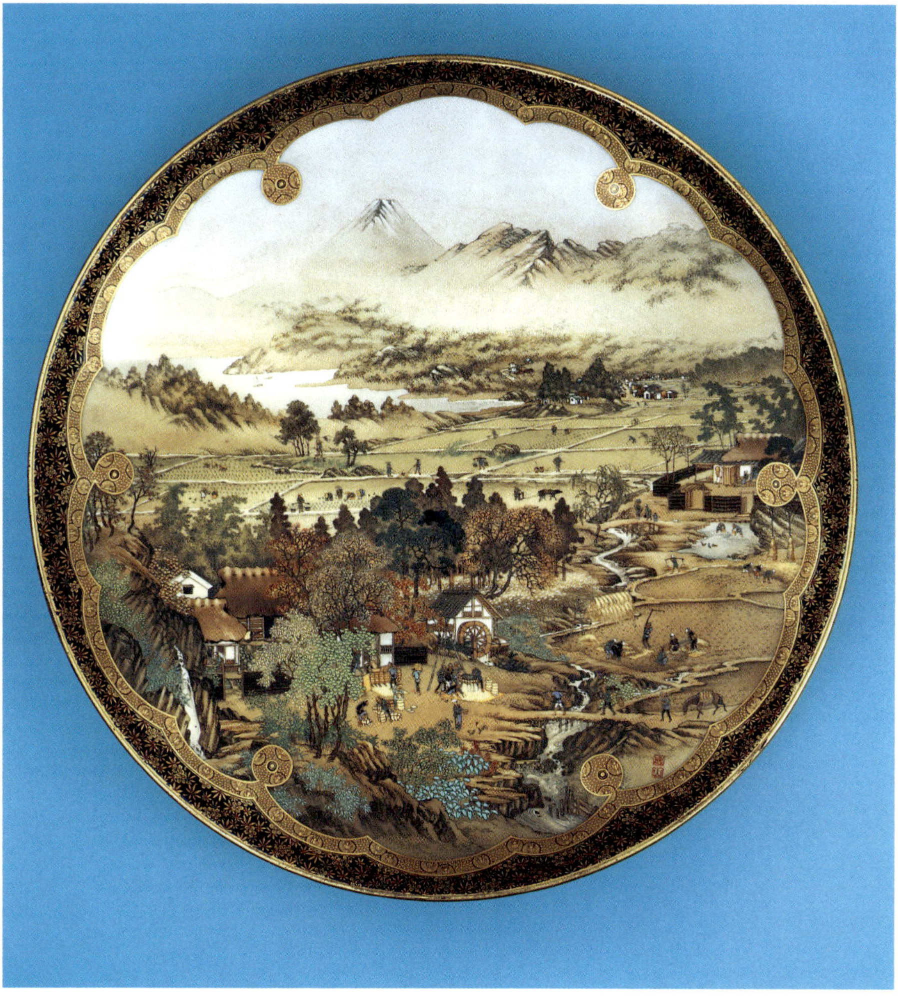

19 Earthenware vase

Reticulated, chrysanthemums
By Kinkōzan Sōbei VII
Sealed
1900–1905
H. 30.0 cm

Story Fund 1997.41

Earthenware vase pierced and modelled with large and small chrysanthemum flowers and leaves glazed in natural colours. It is presumed that this formerly had a lid. Impressed seal on base: *Kinkōzan zō*.

At the Exposition Internationale in Paris in 1900, Japanese crafts were badly mauled by the critics as out-of-date, over decorated, and for the fact that the decoration did not reflect the shape; the Japanese had failed to notice the progression of western styles. This was a rude shock to the Japanese who had had such successes previously. In fact this was a somewhat sweeping generalization for cloisonné enamel, for instance, had developed along western lines. But ceramics had often lagged behind (see the comment on Yabu Meizan's exhibits in 1910). And yet Japan was both an influence upon as well as being influenced by *art nouveau* as is very evident here. This reticulated vase is only about five years later than the plate described above (no.18). A somewhat similar vase was exhibited at the International Exposition in St. Louis in 1904.

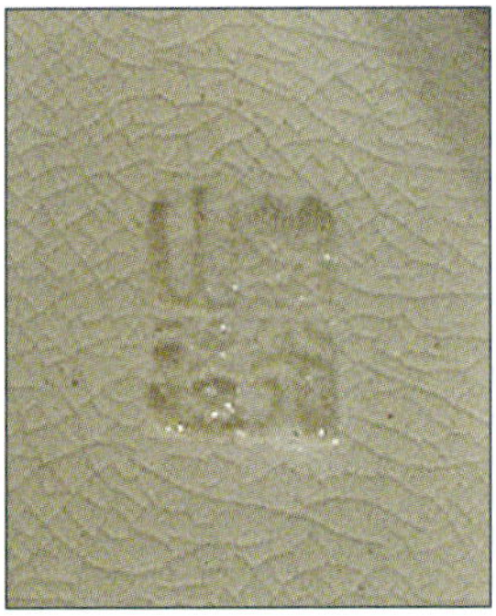

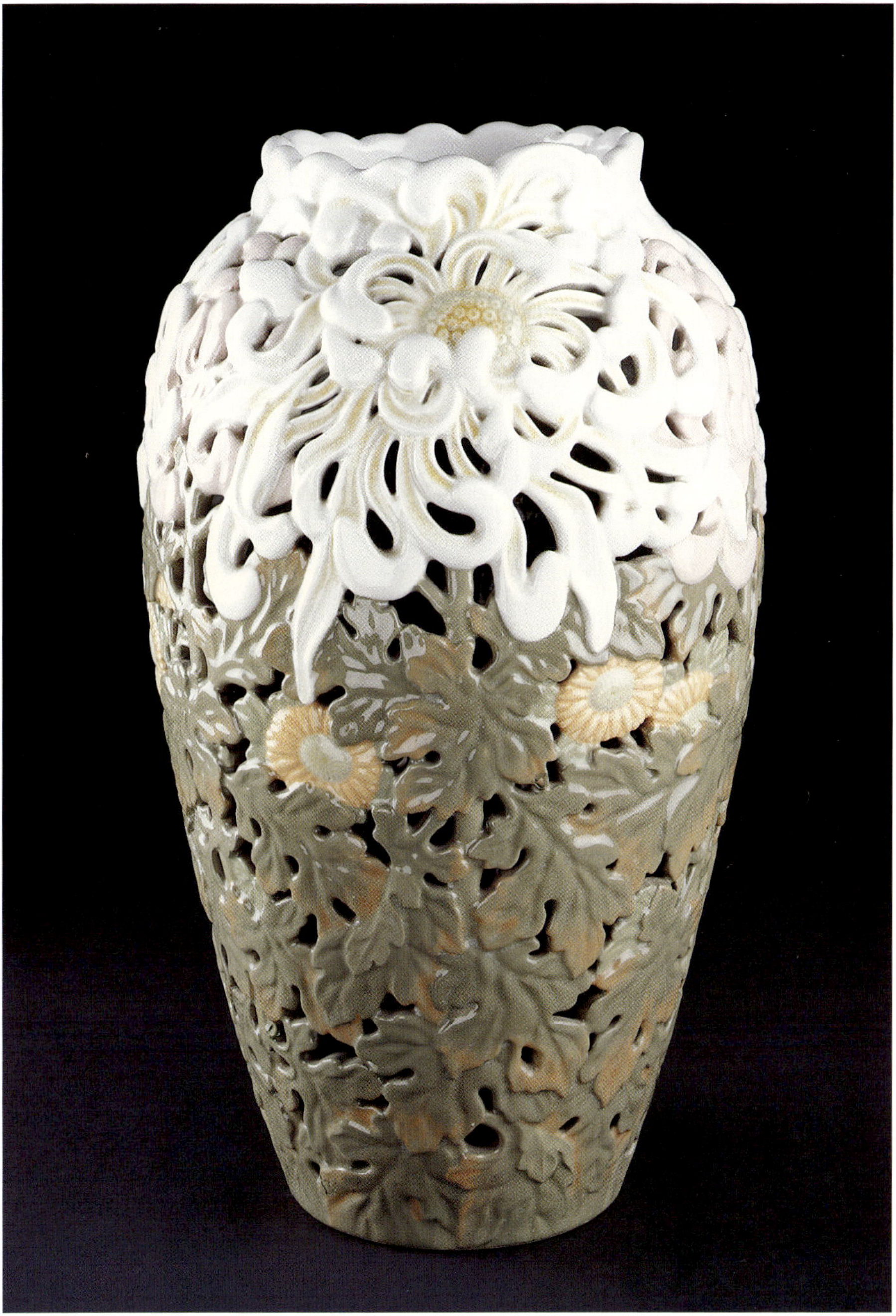

20 Earthenware squared vase

Scenes in cartouches, overglaze enamel and underglaze blue
By Hōzan
The images by Shunkei
c. 1890
H. 32.4 cm

Gift of Mrs. Ruth van Heyningen
1990.1237

Earthenware vase of square section with everted neck and painted borders on neck and shoulders. The sides elaborately enamelled with scenes of women and children and flowers and animals. Seal on base: *Kyōto Hōzan*. Each painted panel signed: *Shunkei* with different seals: *Uzaki*.

As the so-called Satsuma style in Kyōto increased in sophistication in such examples as this, and at the factory of Kinkōzan, the individual painters often signed their better work, though we lack information on their identities.

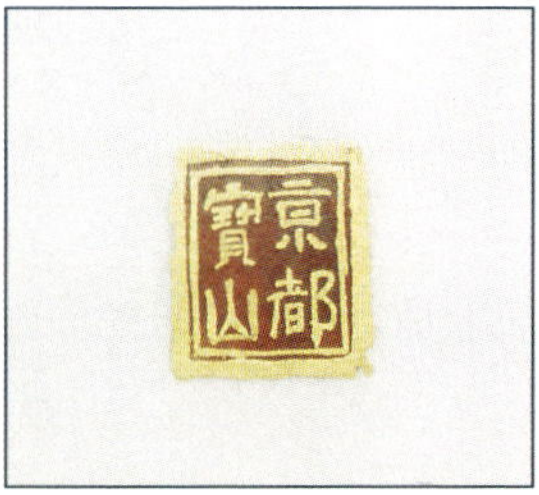

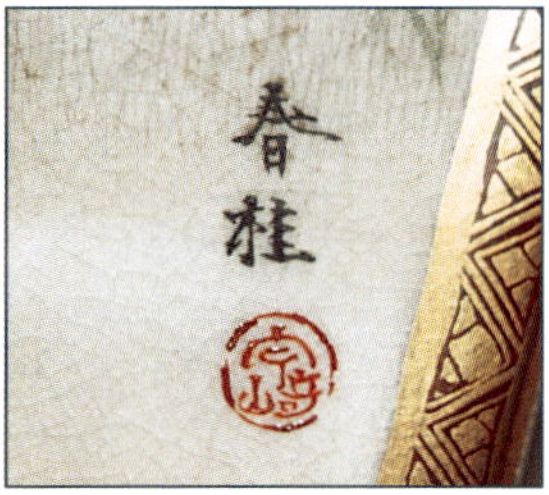

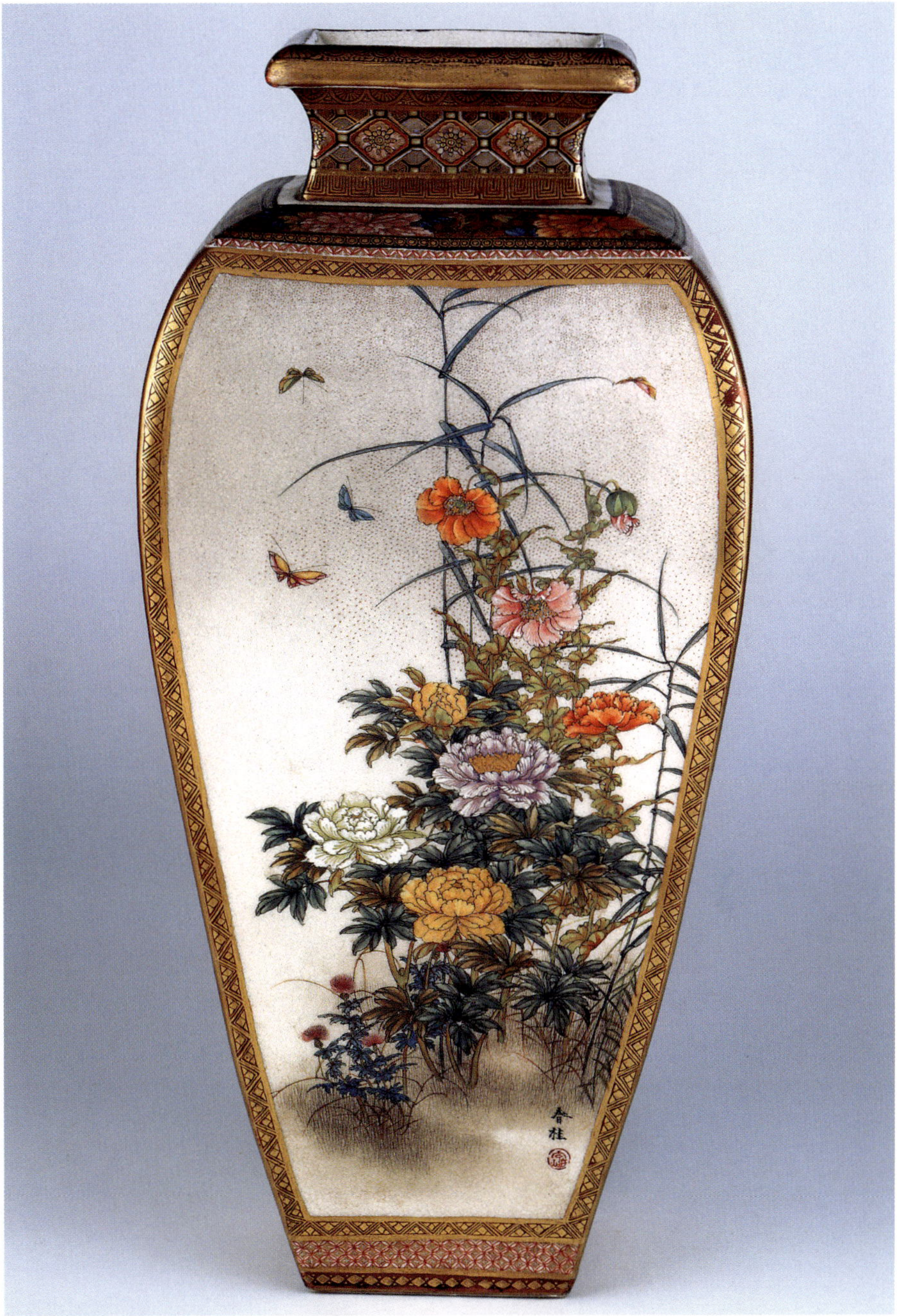
春桂

21 Earthenware vase

By Yabu Meizan
Overglaze enamels, bird and spider
Signed
c. 1910
H. 24.7 cm

Story Fund 1993.12

Earthenware vase decorated with a bird perched on a flowering cherry tree, watching a spider descending on a thread among autumn leaves. Signed on the base with the seal-mark: *Yabu Meizan.*

Yabu Meizan (1853–1934) was a decorator, not a potter; the ceramic body was bought in as a blank, probably from Kagoshima. His factory in Ōsaka produced Satsuma-style overglaze-decorated pieces, specialising in the minute depiction of large numbers of figures in processions. For this, he used copper templates many of which have survived, though their use is extremely difficult to detect. At the Japan-British Exhibition at Shepherd's Bush in 1910, he exhibited pieces both in his old style, and in a new, much more open style, such as that of the vase here. While the critics praised the new style ('contemporary'), the public preferred the old style even though it was very expensive.

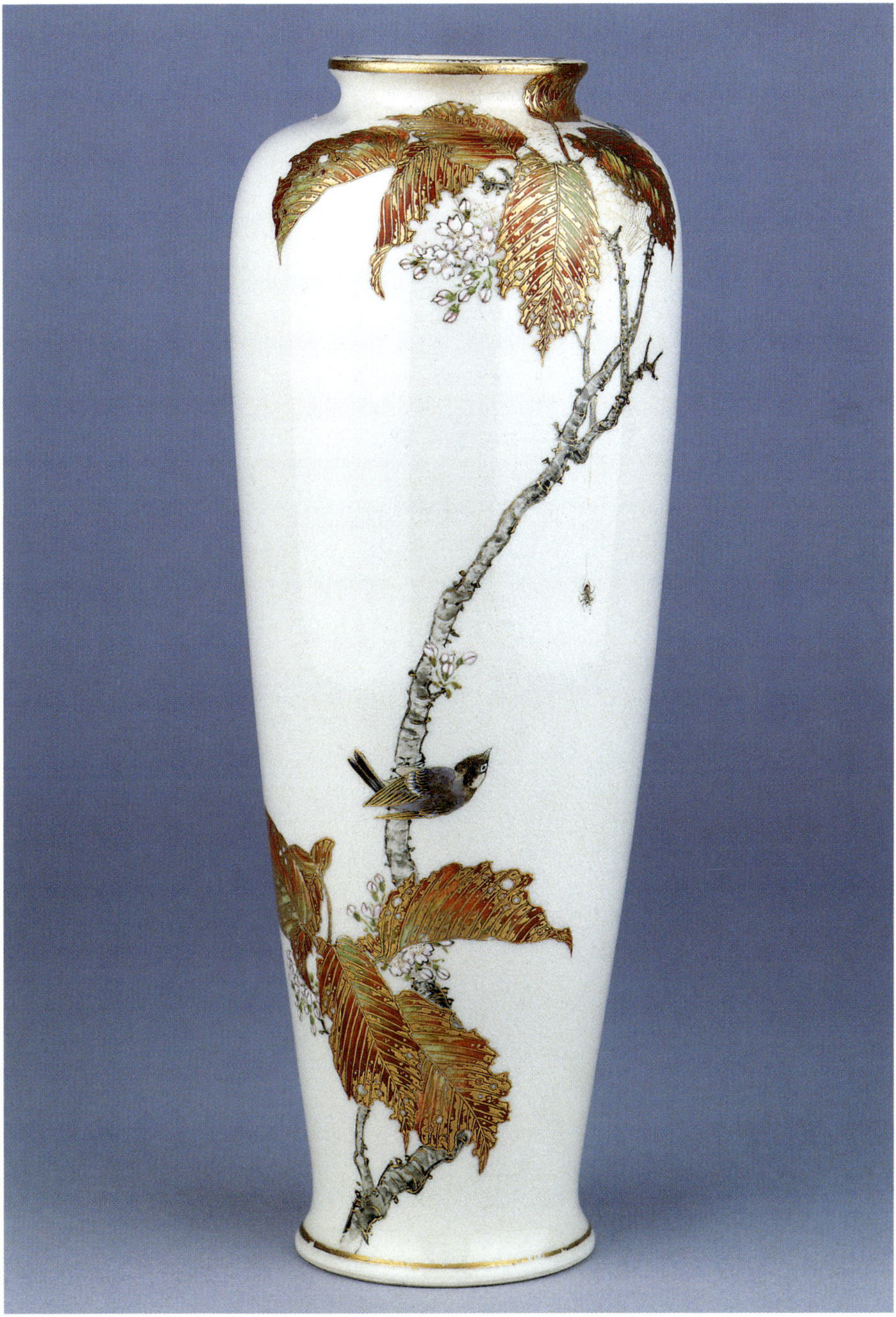

22 Earthenware cup

By Tōkōzan
Kumamoto kiln, Kagoshima, Kyūshū
Signed
Early 20th century (before 1908)
H. 7.5 cm Gift of Sir Herbert Ingram 1956.681

Straight sided earthenware cup with a chrysanthemum spray in soft enamels beneath a key-fret border, all over a finely crackled ivory glaze. Signed in gold on side: *Satsuma Tōkōzan sei*, with a square red seal.

In spite of arguments to the contrary (some of them very heated) it seems clear that the enamelled Satsuma wares, sometimes called 'brocaded wares' were first made at Kagoshima, in the Satsuma domain, in the middle of the nineteenth century and were imitated in other areas of Japan (Tōkyō, Kyōto, Ōsaka, Yokohama etc.) later.

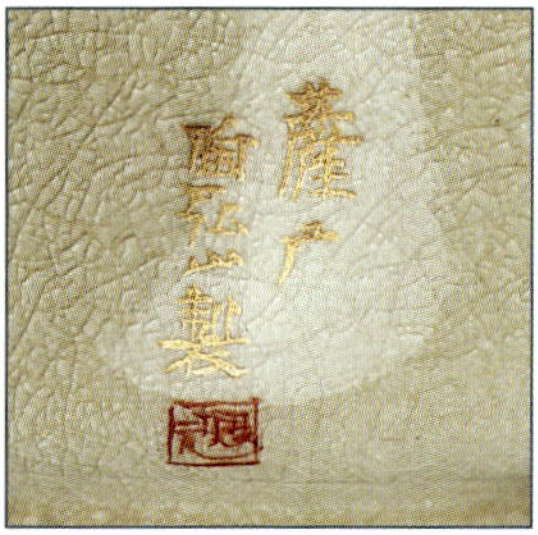

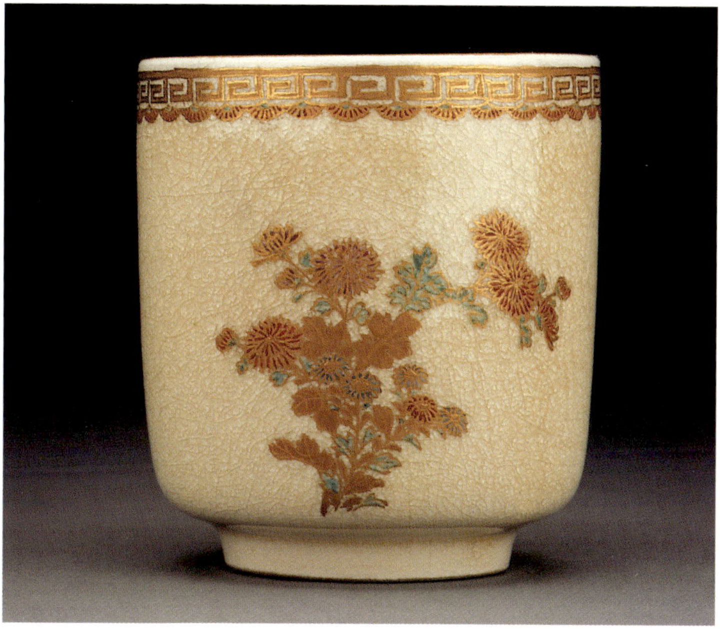

23 Earthenware bowl

Attributed to Chin Jukan XII
Chin Jukan Workshop, Naeshirogawa, Kyūshū
Unsigned
c 1900 (before 1908)
H. 9.0 cm: W. 12.3 cm

Gift of Sir Herbert Ingram 1956.3987

Earthenware teabowl decorated over a matt translucent glaze, in coloured enamels, with fourteen different shaped cartouches containing flowers, birds and figures, all against a gold *sayagata* ground. The interior with a fierce coiled dragon among clouds.

This bowl can be firmly attributed to the Chin Jukan workshop, by comparison with the decoration on the pair of large vases made for the World's Columbian Exhibition of Chicago in 1893, by Chin Jukan XII, which have similar floral cartouches on an identical gold *sayagata* background. This attribution has been confirmed by the present Chin Jukan XV.

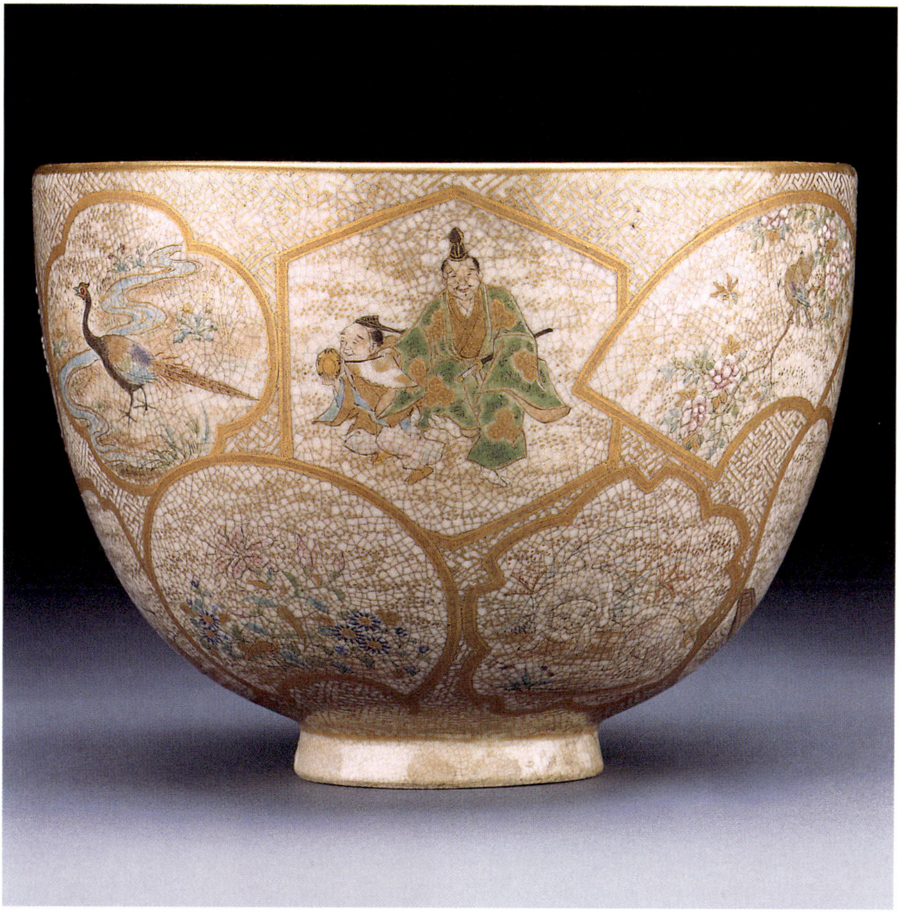

24 One of a pair of vases

Bronze and soft metal inlay
By Kanamori Tokitsugu
Signed
1870s
H. 64.0 cm X 5148 & X 5149

One of a pair of vases in bronze and soft metals, each made in six parts. The base a flat platform on which sits a tripod stand with phoenix shaped feet, with pierced panels of drums, gourds and scrolls, with applied *daikon* (radish). This supports a hexagonal gallery on which rests a bulbous vase with short neck and large, flattened tray-like rim, with upright sides. Each vase bears two shaped panels on the sides containing different scenes - a courtier on a horse fording a stream, a bird on a rock beside bamboo, a courtier with two attendants and a bird flying through a bamboo grove beside rocks. On the flat surface of the rim, spools and skeins of thread with applied 'Chinese lantern' (*Physalis*) seed pods. Engraved signature within one vase: *Kanamori Tokitsugu sei*.

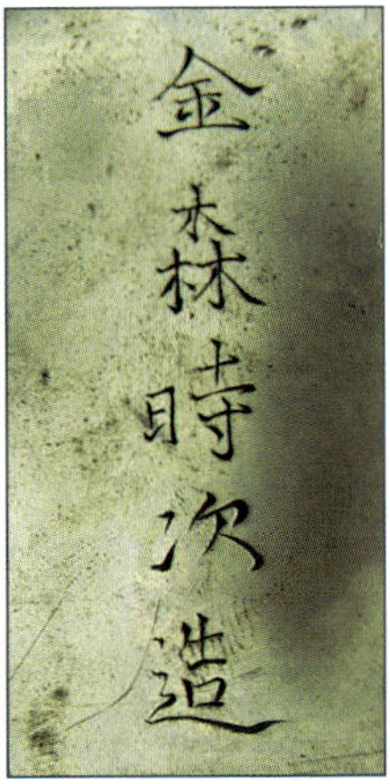

Based on a classic flower-vase shape, this elaborate concoction, typical of the higher quality work of the Kaga metalworkers of early Meiji Japan, looks as if it was designed by a committee; it probably was. Kanamori Tokitsugu appears to be otherwise unrecorded. Almost certainly made by a small group of former sword-fittings makers, this bears decoration piled on decoration and stands on a series of extra supporting plinths and feet, in the search for elaboration and the demonstration of skill that was the reaction of Japanese craftsmen of the time to High Victorianism. It is likely that the vases were made for one of the great International Expositions of the time, perhaps Vienna (1873), Philadelphia (1876) or Paris (1878), but we have found no record.

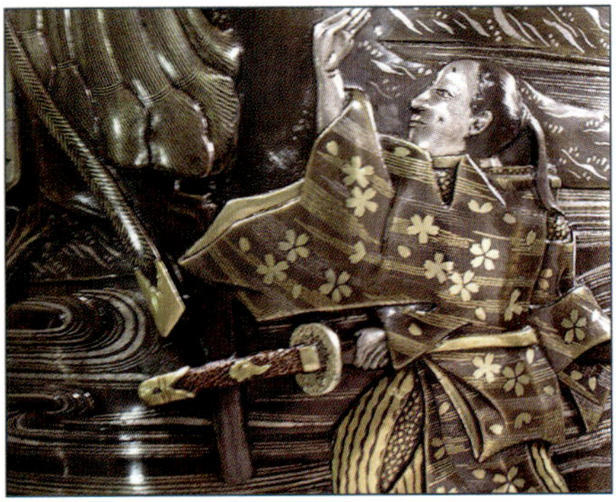

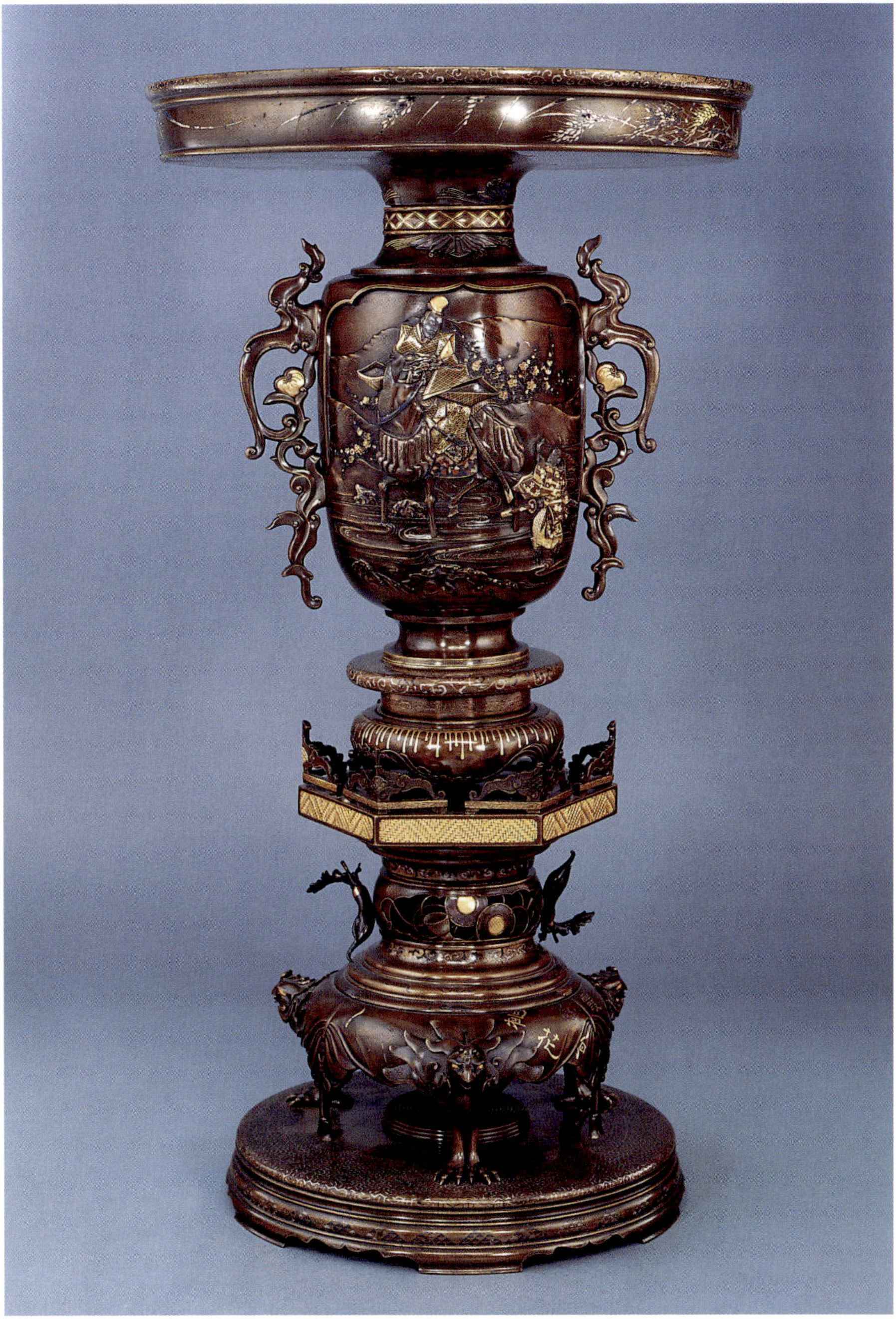

25 Dish

Bronze with soft metal inlay
By the Komai Company
Signed
c. 1885
D. 35.5cm

Story Fund 1995.116

Bronze, gold and silver lobed dish with central relief panel of a bearded Chinese warrior in *shakudō*, silver and gold *nunome-zōgan*. The body of the dish with layers of radiating petal-shapes similarly inlaid in gold *nunome-zōgan* in various geometric patterns and scattered cherry blossoms and butterflies, the ground with silver stars, the border with vines. Signed on reverse: *Nihon koku Kyōto jū Komai sei.*

The Komai Company was one of the specialist metalworking companies that descended from a sword-fittings company. Originally founded in 1841, the company did not start to make the inlaid works for which the company drew its reputation until the time of the founder's grandson, Komai Otojirō I (1842–1917), at around the time when the wearing of swords was banned in Meiji Japan in 1876. The company's name rarely appears in Exposition catalogues because of an agreement with the important commissioning company of Ikeda Seisuke, under whose name any Komai objects would be exhibited. His shop was first in Shinmonzen and later in Furumonzen, the haunts of foreign clients in Kyōto.

The company specialised in the making of bronze vases and dishes inlaid in *zōgan* technique in gold and silver. Dishes characteristically have a central motif with a large figure design, surrounded by pattern-making inlays, and frequently bordered by a vine pattern.

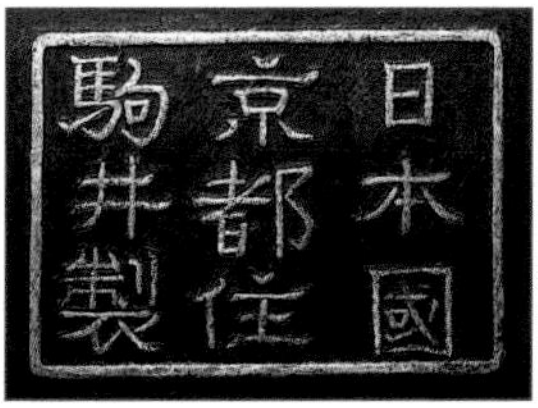

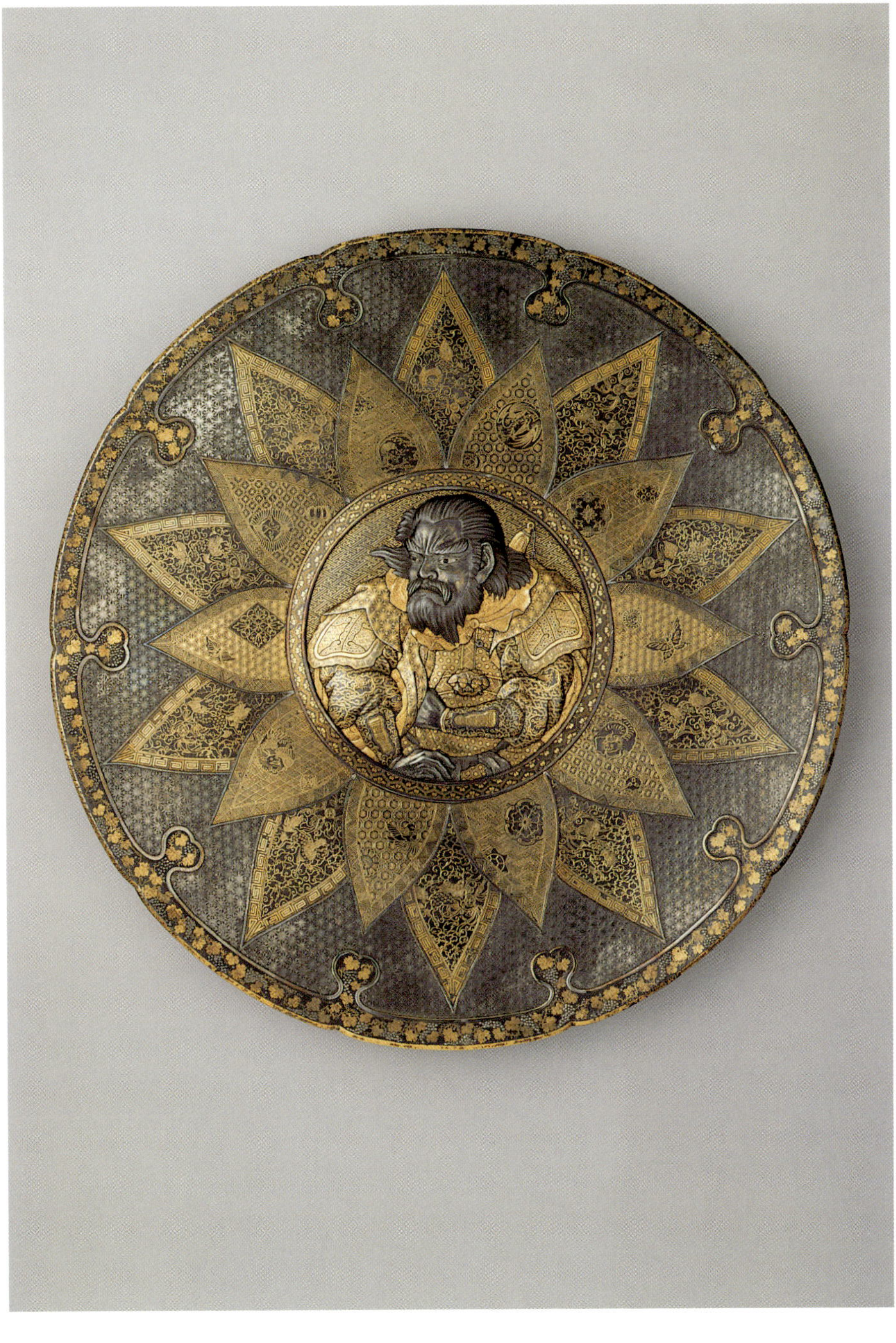

26 Vase

Bronze with soft metal inlay and cloisonné enamel
By Takasaki Kōichi
Signed
1890s
H. 18.0 cm

Story Fund 1994.109

Baluster vase in silver, *shibuichi*, and cloisonné enamel. The neck in silver with petal-shapes on the shoulder, the body decorated with tree peonies in relief in cloisonné enamel. Engraved signature on exterior: *Hōryūsai Kōichi* with gold inlaid *kakihan* and on the base: *Takasaki Seizo*.

Details of the life of Takasaki Kōichi appear to be unknown; however there exists a group of vases, usually of bronze and silver, and encrusted with *shippō* (cloisonné) inlays in which there is a silver neck that either simulates dripping of a liquid over the bronze or fuses into the bronze in a careful pattern, some of which are signed Takasaki Kōichi, or Hōryūsai Kōichi (as here), which can all be attributed to Kōichi. In the Paris Exposition of 1900, Takasaki Kōichi exhibited a pair of silver vases decorated with peonies and poppies in cloisonné enamel.

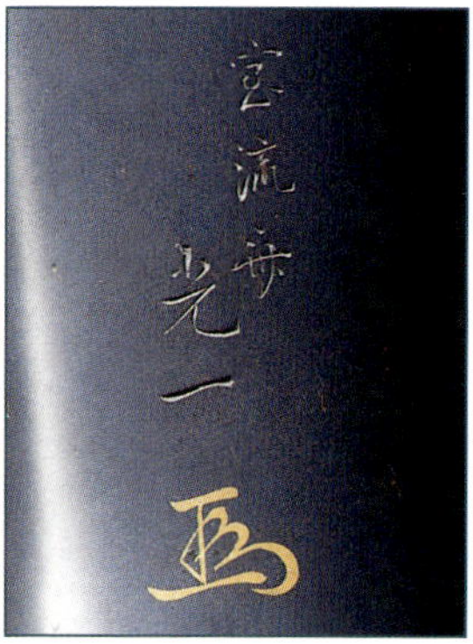

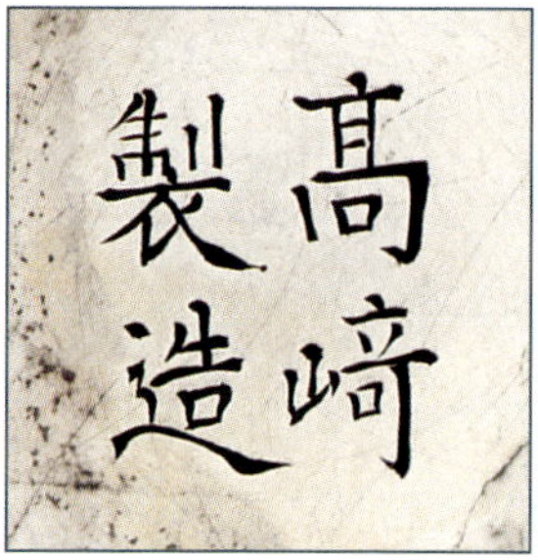

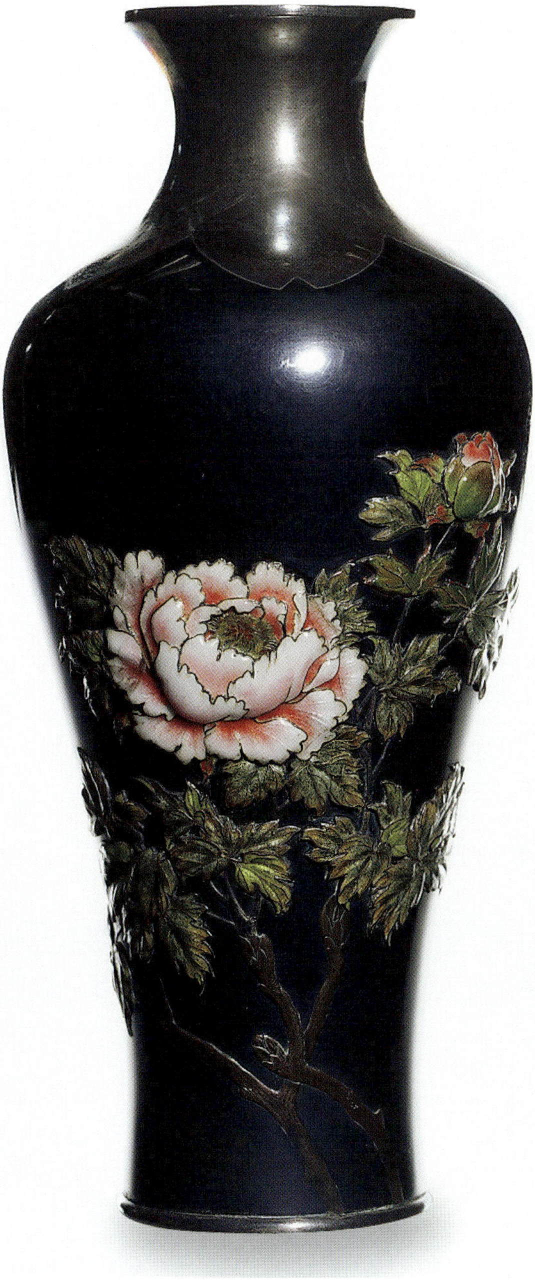

27 Sword-guard

Iron with soft metal inlay
By Kanō Natsuo
Signed
Late 19th century
H. 8.9 cm Oppenheimer gift X 3852

Sword-guard (*tsuba*) of tapered rectangular shape in iron and soft metal with relief decoration of three carp, one leaping the other two swimming, on the reverse, a fourth carp swimming. Engraved signature: *Natsuo* with *kakihan.*

Kanō Natsuo (1828–1898) is usually acknowledged as the finest of the Meiji metalworkers, and, indeed one of the finest metalworkers of Japan of any period. He studied the making of sword-fittings, and later studied painting under the Shijō painter Nakajima Raishō (1796–1871). Winner of almost every prize available to metalworkers in the National Industrial Expositions, he was also a judge at the Second, Third and Fourth Expositions. He worked for the National Mint, and in 1890 was created an Imperial Artist.

In all probability this *tsuba*, with its Shijō-derived design of carp, only just falls into our period; sword fittings were made to special order by several metalworkers even after the banning of the wearing of swords in 1876. Natsuo had been commissioned to make (or to decorate) a ceremonial *tachi* (slung sword) in 1871 by the Imperial Household Agency.

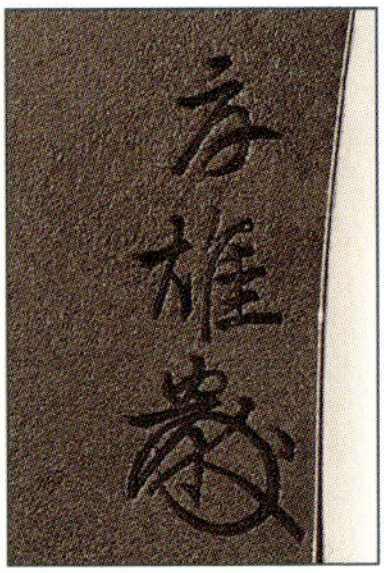

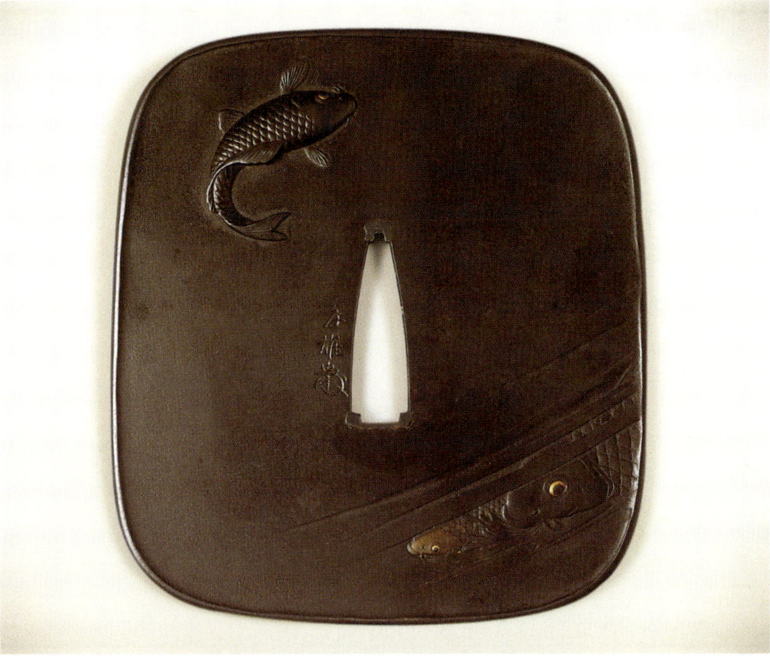

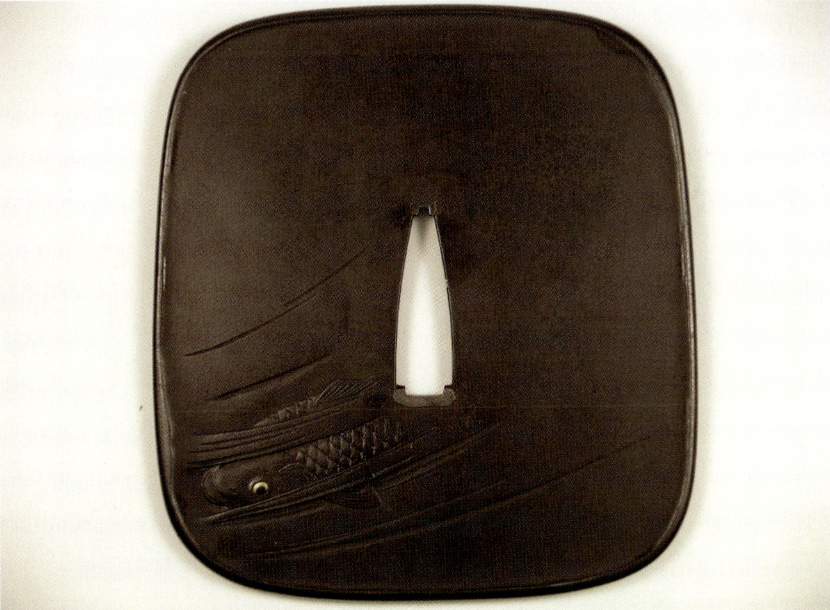

28 Panel

Soft metal alloys
By Unno Shōmin
Signed and sealed
Summer, 1891
W. 40.4 cm

Story Fund 1998.220

Fan-shaped panel in soft metal of two main colours, *shibuichi* and *shakudō*, engraved in *katakiri* with a waterfall. Engraved signature: *Unno Shōmin koku*. Seal: *Hoshu sei*. Dated: *Meiji kanoto natsu no hi* (summer 1891).

Half a generation younger than Kanō Natsuo, and his natural successor, Unno Shōmin (1844–1915) is usually considered the finest Meiji metalworker after Natsuo (see no. 27). He won prizes in many International and National Expositions, and one of his figure studies in the Third National Exposition was purchased by the Imperial Household Agency. He was a professor at the Tōkyō Art School from 1890 and became an Imperial Artist in 1896.

The deep cutting of the engraved panel is a triumph of skill in a difficult process; with a broad chisel this nevertheless achieves a surety of line that is quite remarkable. The juxtaposition of the dark *shakudō* riverbank with the silver waterfall is typical of Shōmin's inventiveness. This is also remarkable for being dated. It would originally have been mounted on a framed panel of *kiri* wood (*Paulownia*), probably without glass.

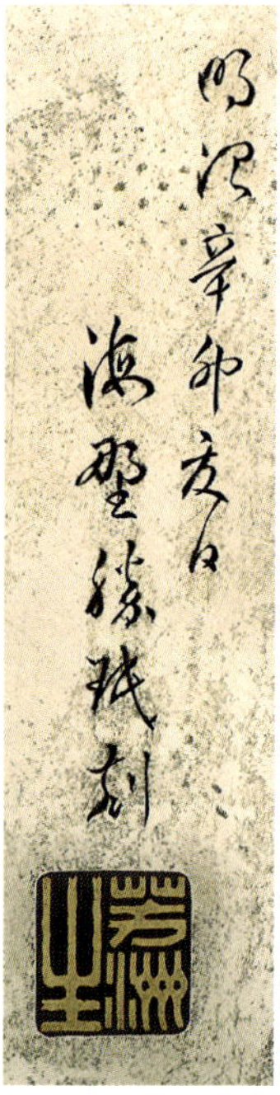

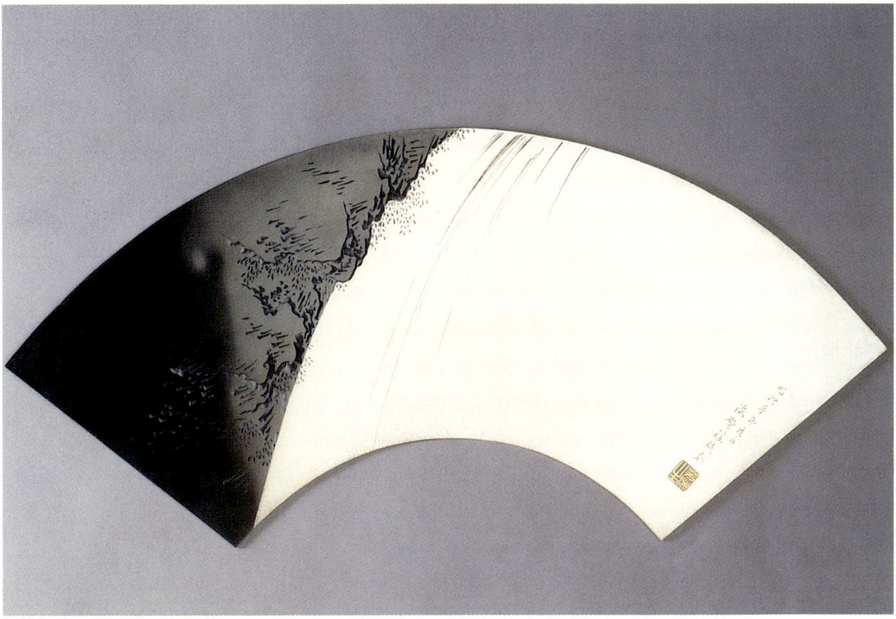

29 Plaque

Soft metal alloys set in a lacquer box
By Kajima Ikkoku II
Signed
c. 1910
H. 7.5 cm: w. 5.4 cm

Gift of Sir Herbert Ingram 1956.1787

Soft metal plaque with a duck swimming past reeds. Set into the lid of a plain black lacquer box.
Engraved signature: *Ikkokusai.*

Kajima Ikkoku II (1846–1925), who worked in Tōkyō, was the eldest son of Ikkoku I (*c.* 1820–1882) and was called Mitsutaka until his father's death, when he inherited the name. His *gō* was *Ikkokusai*. He won a Certificate of Merit at the Third National Industrial Exposition of 1890 and exhibited both at the St. Louis Exposition in 1904 and at the Japan-British Exhibition in 1910 where his work was illustrated in the catalogue, no. 199, a vase with *nunome* decoration, and no. 200, a double-fan-shaped incense box.

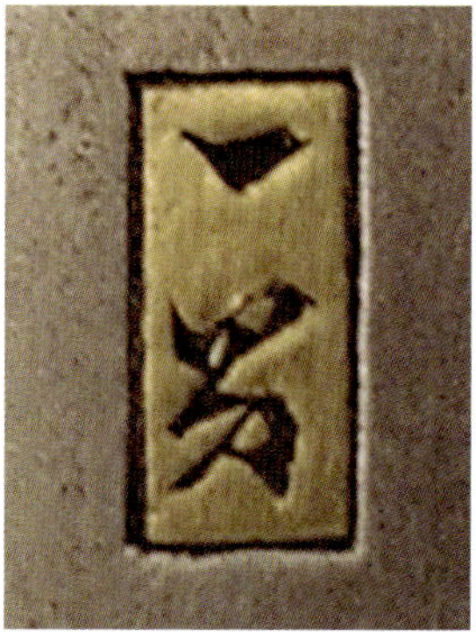

This miniature masterpiece was purchased in Japan by Sir Herbert Ingram on his honeymoon in 1908, for 30 *yen*, as 'box in metal after design by Watanabe' This refers to the artist Watanabe Seitei who supplied designs for several artists or companies, most notably the cloisonné company of Namikawa Sōsuke, see nos. 44, 46 and 47. The image here is quite consistent with his style, and even without the documentation, would have been attributed to Seitei. Ingram was a major benefactor of the Ashmolean and the high quality of his Japanese collections has been overshadowed by his remarkable Chinese collections, given in 1956.

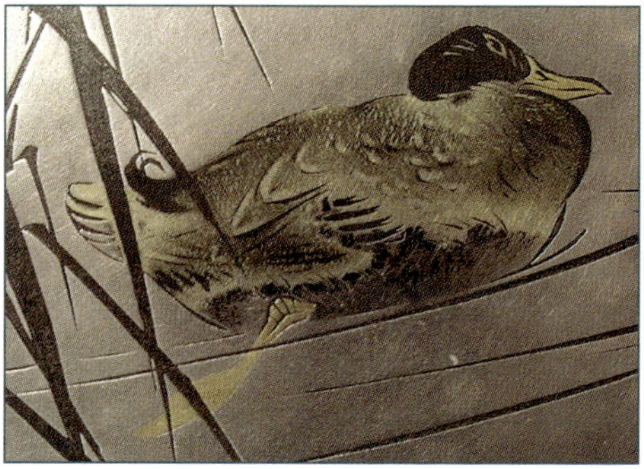

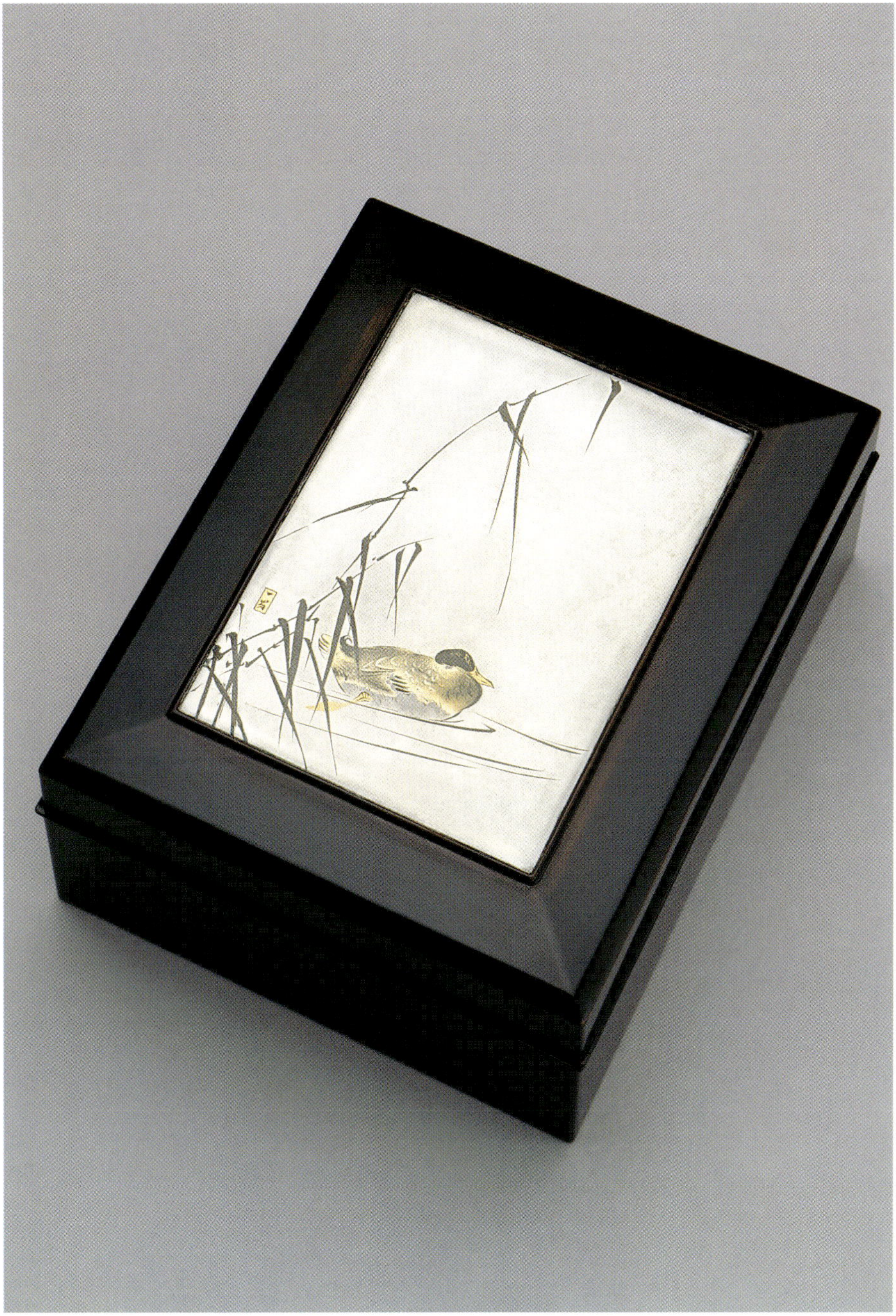

30 Panel

Copper with soft metal inlays
By Yotsuya Seibi
c. 1930
H. 30.0 cm: W. 15.0 cm (in frame)

Story Fund 1997.193

Copper panel inlaid and carved with a mask of Okina lying on a spray of chrysanthemums and daisies. Engraved signature: *Yotsuya Seibi* with gold inlaid seal.

The silver has been cut here to shine, brilliant-cutting, and is preserved with its original lack of patina by the fact that it is glazed and hence free from the tarnish due to oxidation. The maker is little known, but clearly was a pupil of one of the great masters, possibly Unno Shōmin at Tōkyō Art School. Although technically too late for our period, it is illustrated here as an example of the continuation of Meiji craftsmanship well into the Taishō period.

The frame and mounts are original.

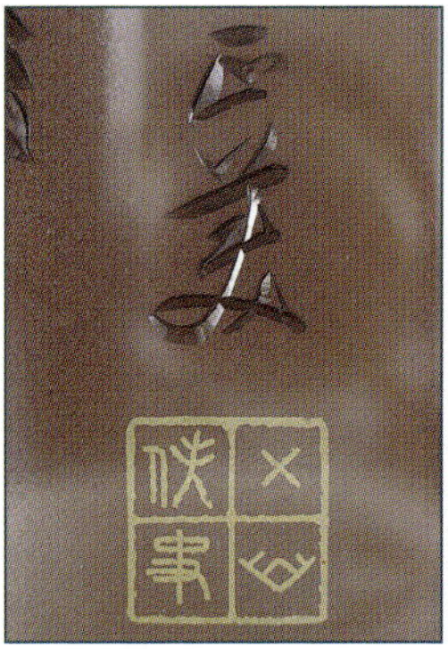

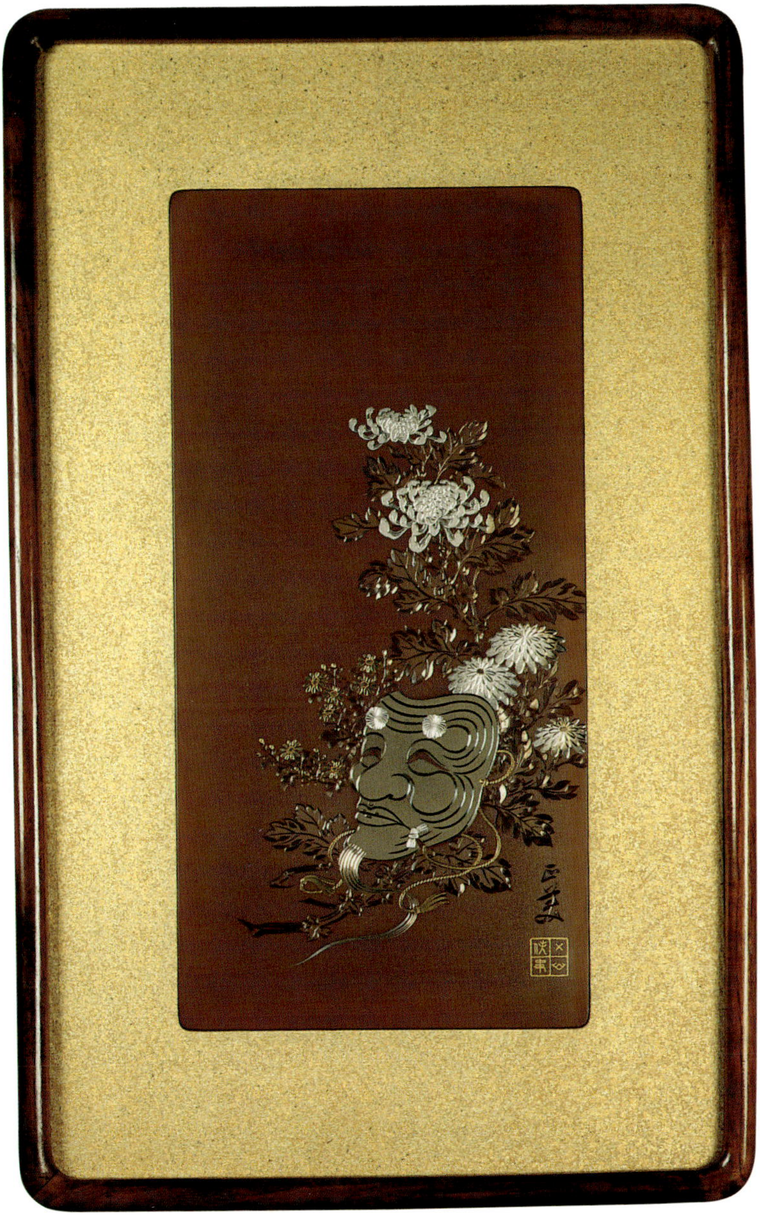

31 Vase

Bronze with soft metal inlay
By Hayashibe Katsunao
Signed and sealed
1900
H. 17.0 cm

Story Fund 1994.65

Baluster shaped bronze vase inlaid in soft metals with a bear on a rock overlooking a stream, in low relief and flat inlay (*hira-zōgan*). Engraved signature: *Hayashibe Katsunao* with inlaid gold seal: *Nao*.

No other works by this artist seem to be recorded. This vase was exhibited at the Paris Exposition Internationale in 1900, and illustrated in the catalogue (unnumbered and unpaginated). Similar such vases, by a number of different artists, were exhibited at the same Exposition.

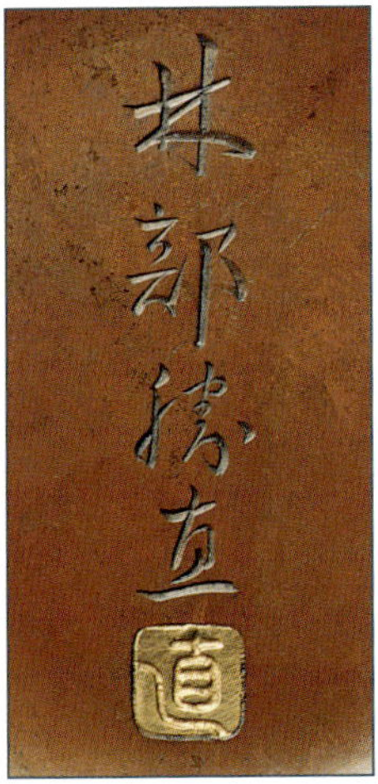

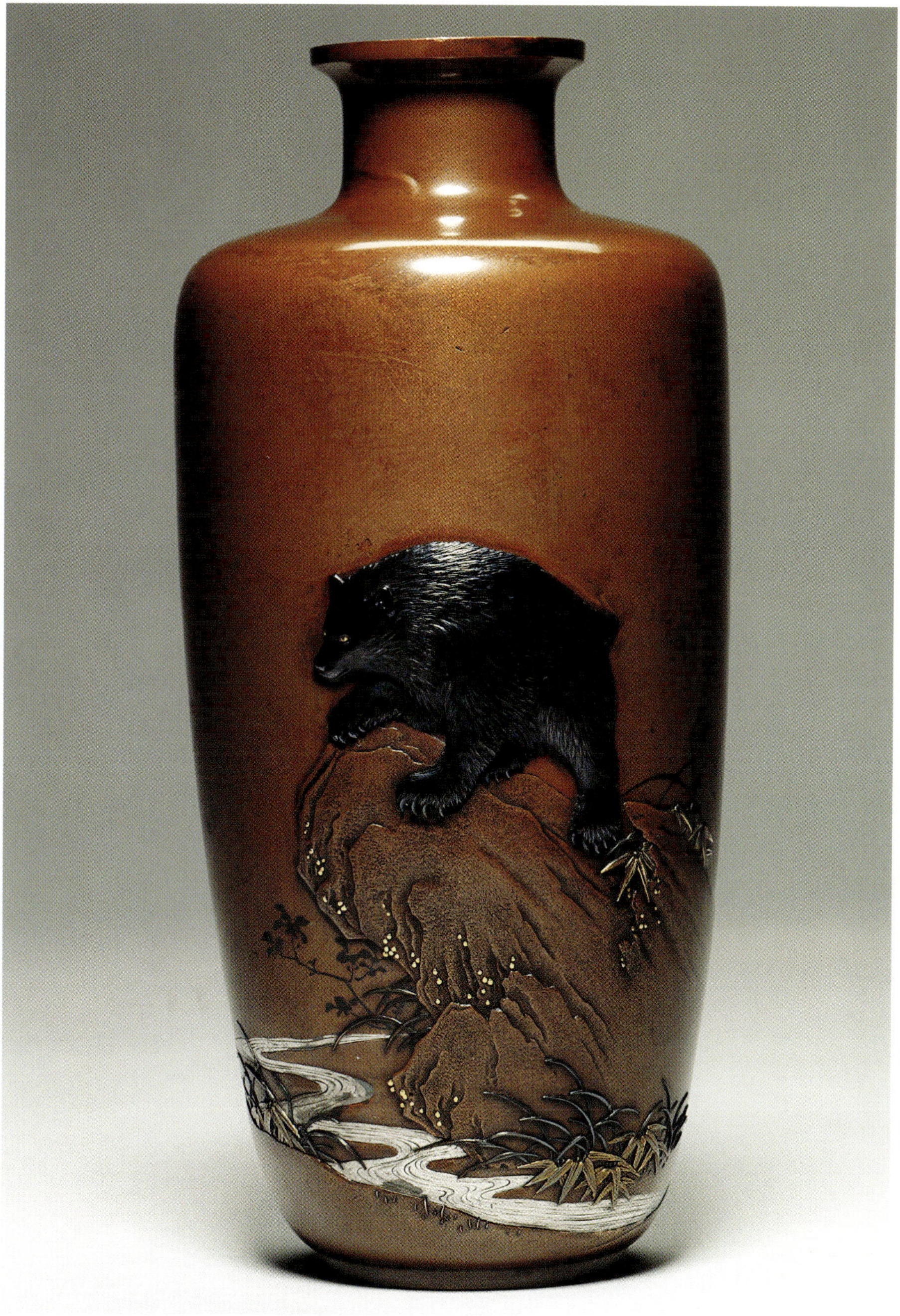

32 Seated figure

Bronze and wood
By Udagawa Kazuo
Signed
Early 20th century
H. 58.cm: Story Fund 1989.14

Bronze figure of a woman cradling a baby on her knee. She holds chopsticks in her right hand and is stretching out to reach a food box (*bentō*) containing rice, placed on a cloth beside her. She sits on a rustic wooden bench with her bare feet on the ground. Signed underneath: *Udagawa Kazuo saku.*

The mother has presumably just finished breast-feeding her baby, and is now eating her lunch from her *bentō* box. The naturalism sought by the sculptors trained at the Tōkyō Art School, where Natsuo (no. 27) and Shōmin (no. 28) taught traditional metalworking skills, was much influenced by the Italian sculptor Vincenzo Ragusa (1841–1927), an *oyatoi gaijin*, one of the foreign 'experts' invited by the Japanese government to advise on various western skills. Carving in wood and ivory was taught, as well as casting in bronze.

Udagawa Kazuo seems to be unrecorded except for his authorship of this fine bronze, examples of which were exhibited in the St. Louis in 1904, in the Fifth National Industrial Exposition in Kyōto in 1905, and in the Japan-British Exhibition in London in 1910.

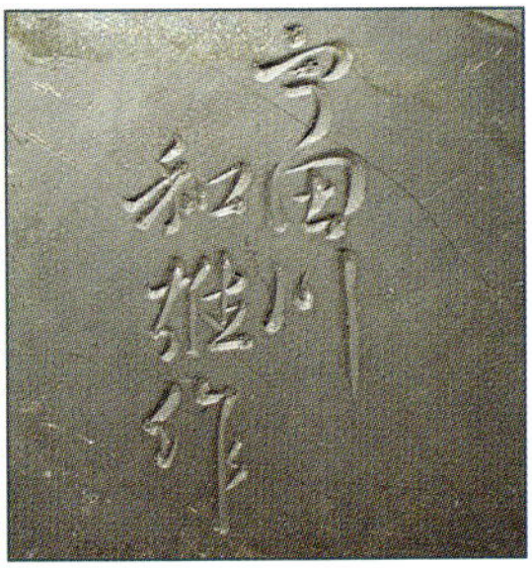

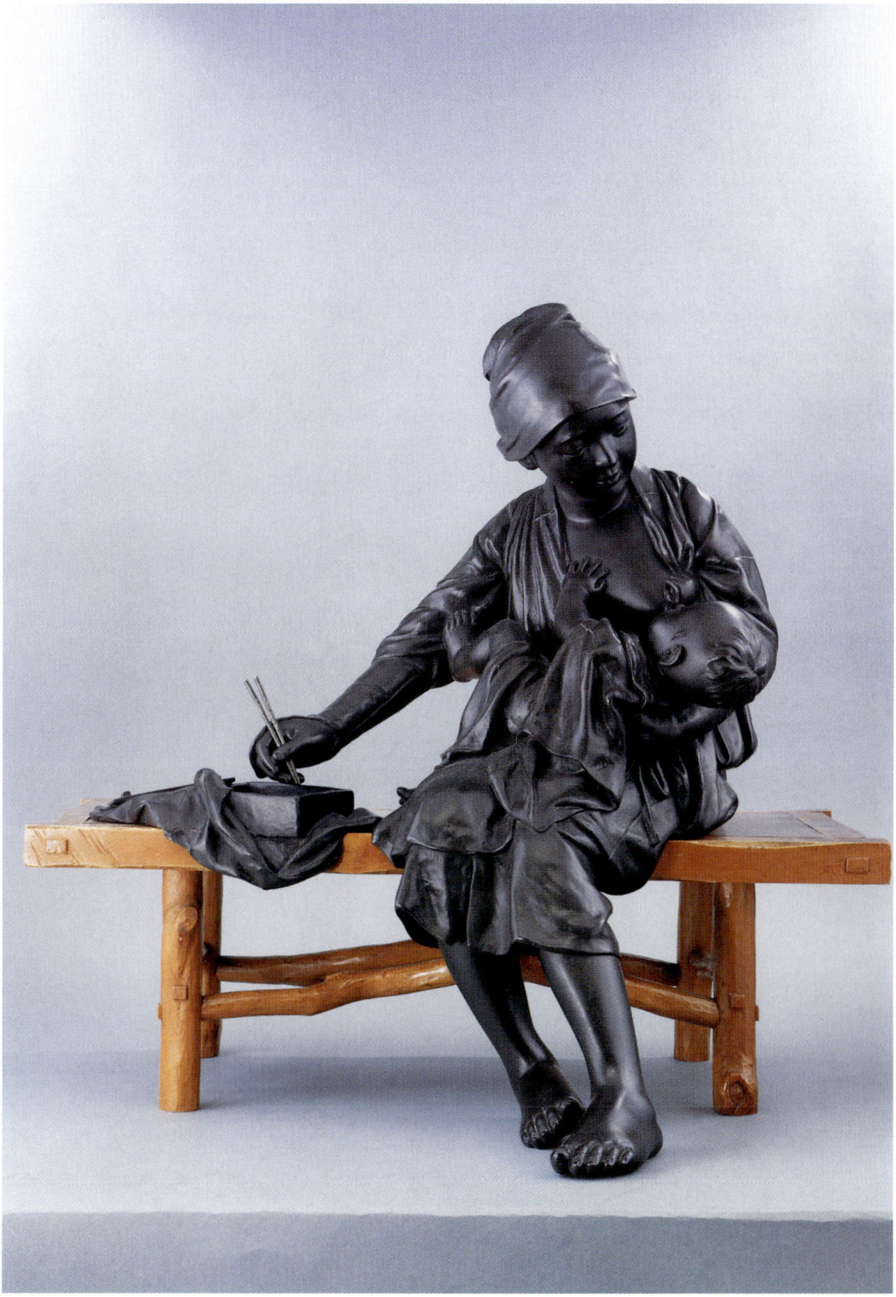

33 Tobacco jar and stand

Cloisonné enamel
By Namikawa Yasuyuki
Unsigned
c. 1880
H. 7.9 cm (jar); W. 7.8 cm (stand)

Story Fund 1995.151

Squared tobacco jar on a flat square tray with butterflies on a yellow ground.

Cloisonné enamel was little used in Japan until the 1830s, when the first three-dimensional objects were made; the early pieces were muddy coloured and much use was made of wire to prevent slippage of the colours. The craft progressed fast and within sixty years was one of the finest of Meiji art-crafts.

The flocculent yellow ground is typical of the work of Namikawa Yasuyuki (1845–1927) in the 1880s; this is simpler than most and must date from early in the decade. The museum owns Yasuyuki's handwritten receipt for this, which gives the day and the month but not, sadly, the year. This receipt enables us to identify other early and unsigned pieces by him.

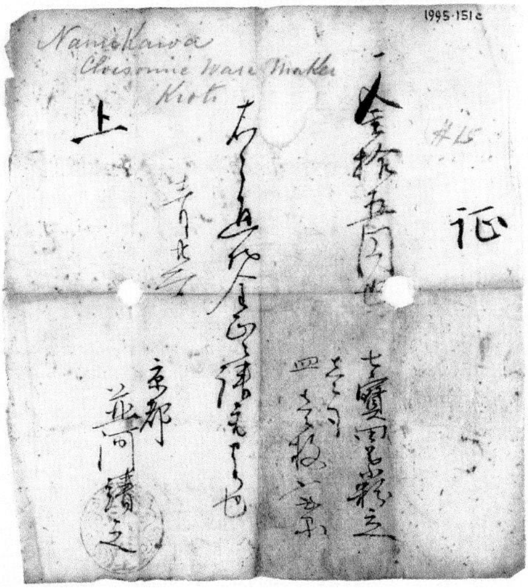

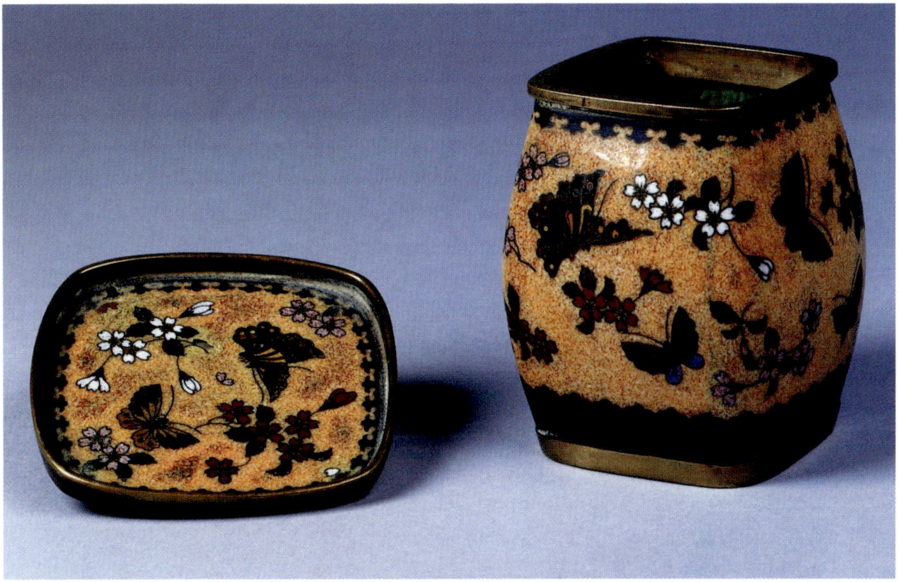

34 Covered jarlet

Cloisonné enamel
Attributed to Namikawa Yasuyuki
Unsigned
1880s
H. 8.5 cm

Story Fund 1993.39

Circular, almost spherical jarlet and cover with three cartouches of birds and flowers on a blue ground, the field scattered with flowers on a black ground. The pierced cover with chrysanthemum-shaped knob and the mounts of copper-gilt.

Although unsigned, for Yasuyuki did not sign his work until a few years later than this, we can confidently attribute this small piece to Yasuyuki. By 1890, he was making dark coloured grounds (apparently more difficult than the yellows and greens), with pictorial elements within wirework cartouches. He was to specialize in fine but not excessive wirework, with gradual lessening of the importance of the borders, and the elimination of the cartouche in favour of tripartite patterns without formal divisions. For this, his work was praised by the perceptive judges of the Fourth National Industrial Exposition in Tōkyō in 1896.

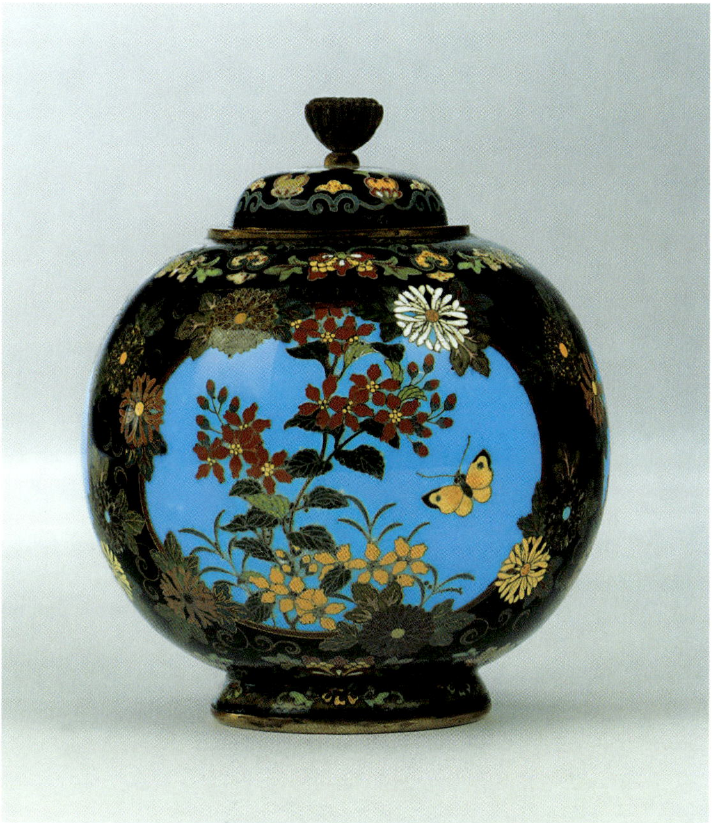

35 Vase

Cloisonné enamel
By Namikawa Yasuyuki
Signed
c. 1900
H. 18.5 cm

Story Fund 1988.1

Vase of slender baluster shape with birds and wisteria flowers in colours and silver wire on a dark blue ground. Silver mounts. Signed on a silver plaque: *Kyōto Namikawa*.

The flowers are balanced all around this vase. After this the next of the stages in the evolution of Yasuyuki's work, shortly after 1900, was the insistence on a front and a back to any vessel; thus there is a main picture as the front and a minimal picture at the back. This leaves a lot of open space unsupported by wire. Frequently the wire is silver, sometimes gold (see no. 37). Borders have been reduced to the minimum, thus emphasising the tall shape. Yasuyuki never used the new exotic techniques that were to be exploited by other artists, preferring to use wire in his own ways (see nos. 36 and 37); here he has actually shaped the 'wire' so that it tapers and alters in thickness as if sculpted. Thus he never used *moriage* (relief, see no. 40) or *plique-à-jour* (unsupported cloisonné, see no. 43), or even the so-called 'wireless' cloisonné (*musen*).

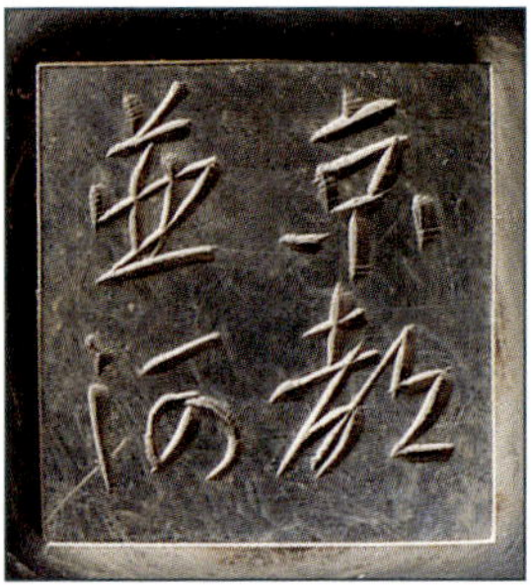

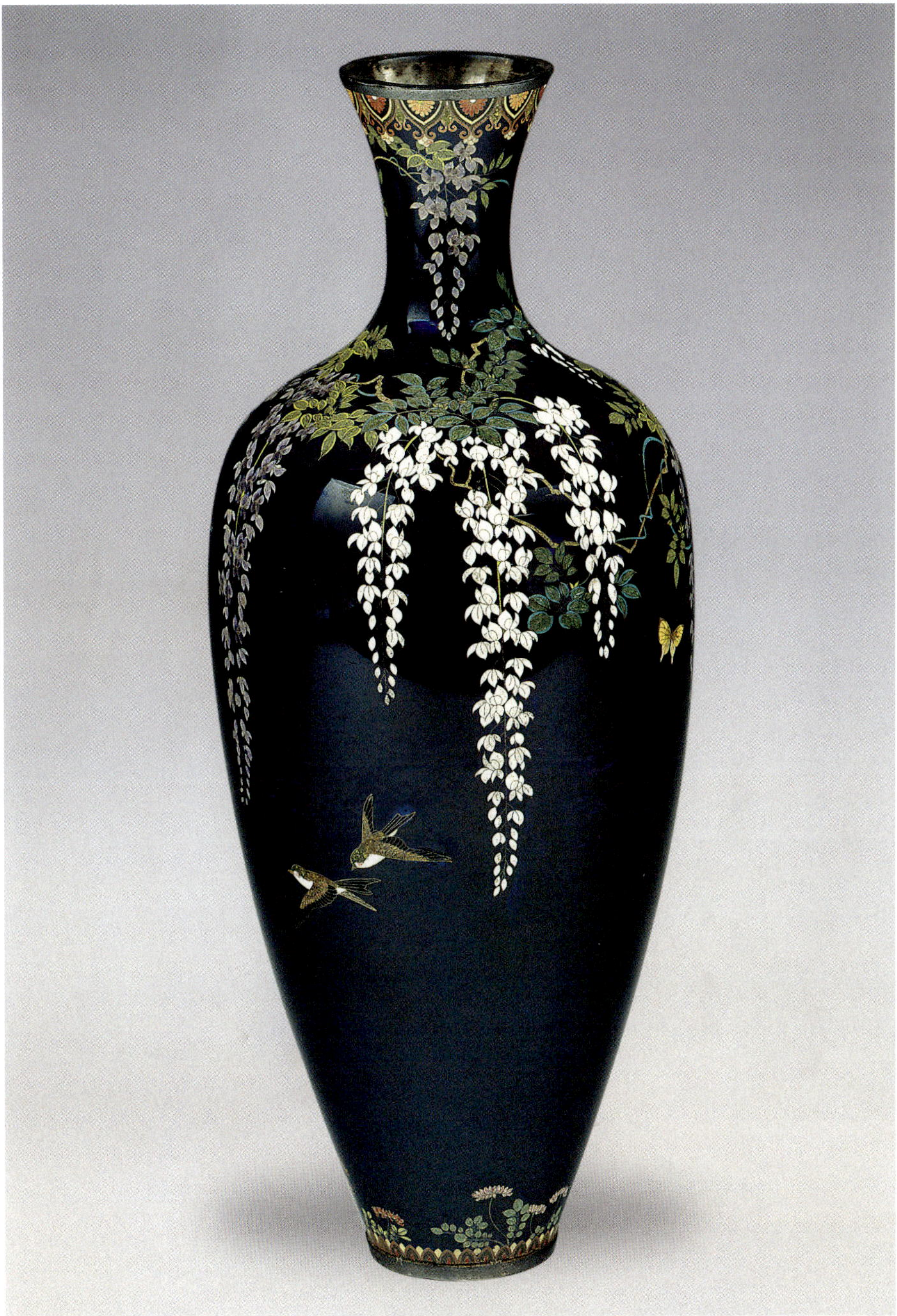

36 Vase

Cloisonné enamel
By Namikawa Yasuyuki
Signed
c. 1903
H. 9.3 cm

Story Fund 2000.48

Small vase of *meiping* shape with chrysanthemums and a butterfly in cut silver and enamel on a pale blue ground. Signed: *Kyōto Namikawa* stamped in the silver base.

In 1903, Yasuyuki's sole entry in the Fifth National Domestic Exposition was a small brush-pot; what confidence! Of this, the judges commented 'the few delicate bamboos look as if they were brush-strokes on a dark purple ground, and each leaf is carved as if it were a brushstroke'. In other words, as can be seen here, Yasuyuki has shaped the 'wire' in almost a reversal of the cloisonné technique, so that the wire becomes a major part of the picture instead of merely outlining the picture. This is the logical next step after the shaping of the wire seen in no. 35.

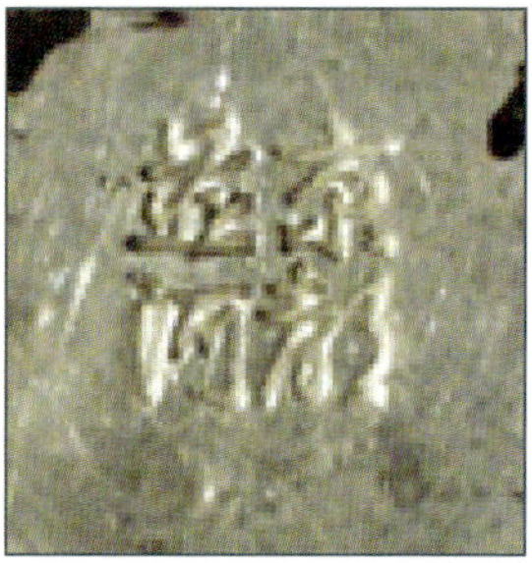

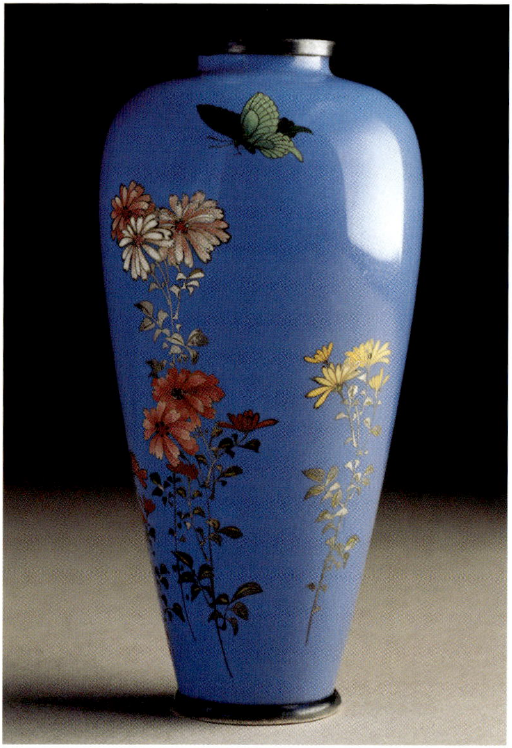

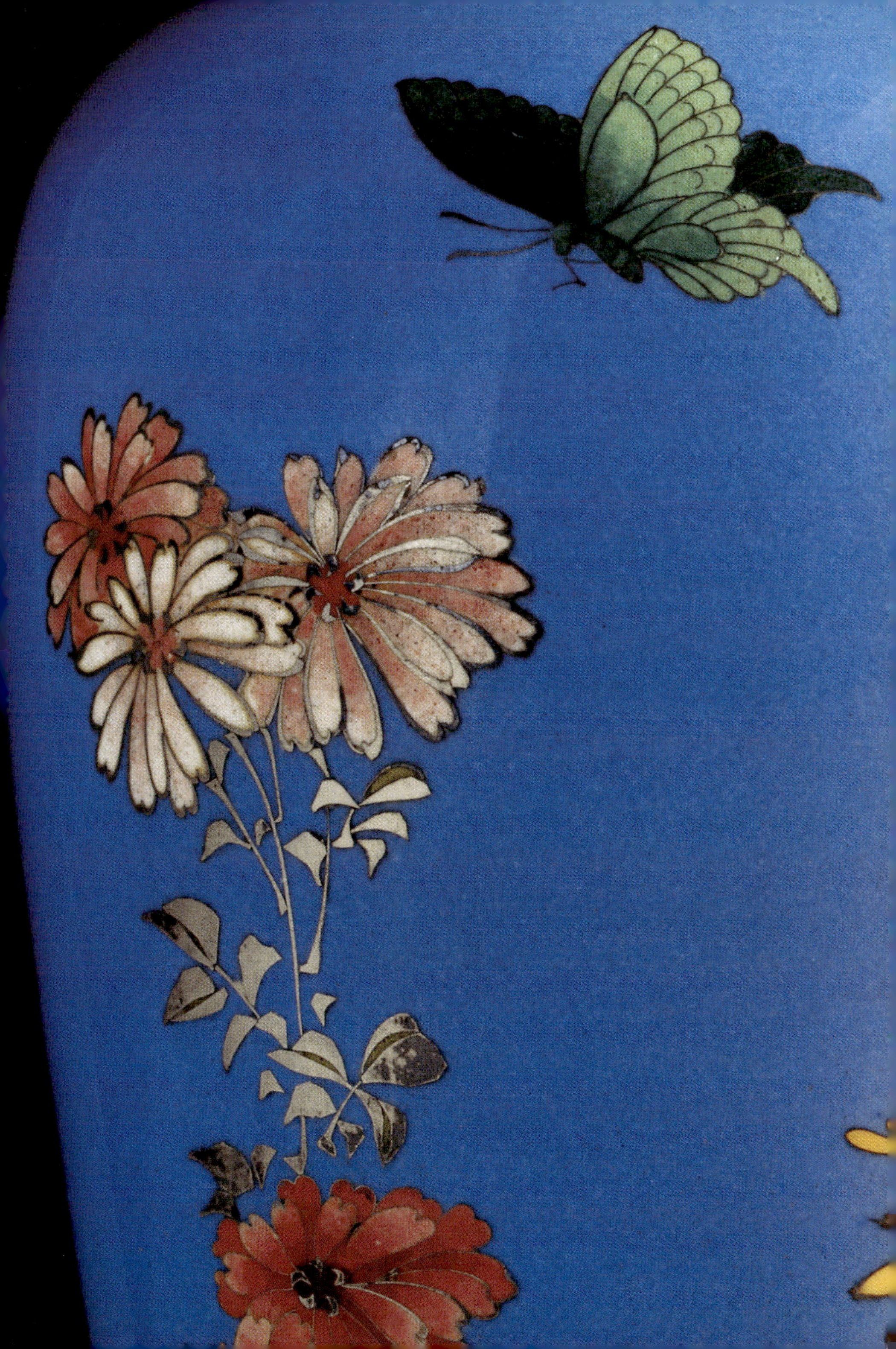

37 Incense Burner

Cloisonné enamel
By Namikawa Yasuyuki
Signed
c. 1905
H. 8.7 cm

Story Fund 2000.180

Baluster shaped incense burner with a lid pierced as a chrysanthemum. A building appears amid trees in a landscape in gold wire on a green ground. Signed; *Kyōto Namikawa* on a silver tablet.

Turning to landscape as a subject, in the early 1900s, Yasuyuki was almost obliged to use shaded backgrounds, which he had usually avoided before. In this gold-wired incense burner, there is another new technique, the use of triangular cross-sections of wire set in the picture end on, to act as leaves or flower-petals.

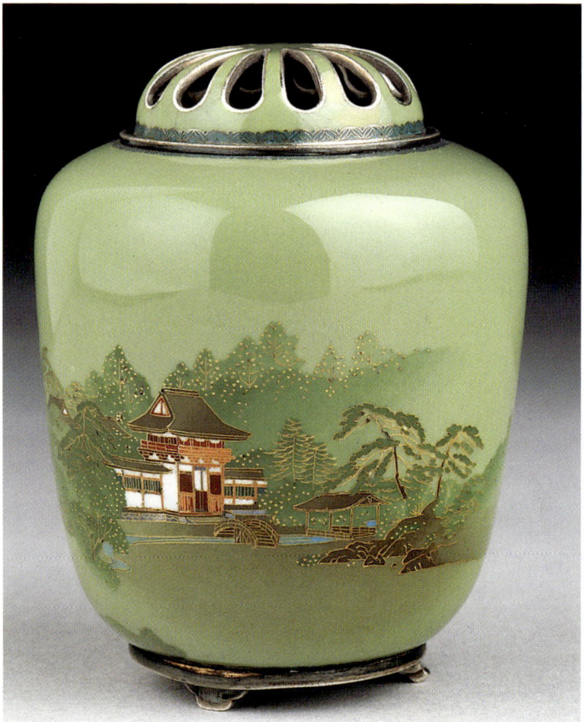

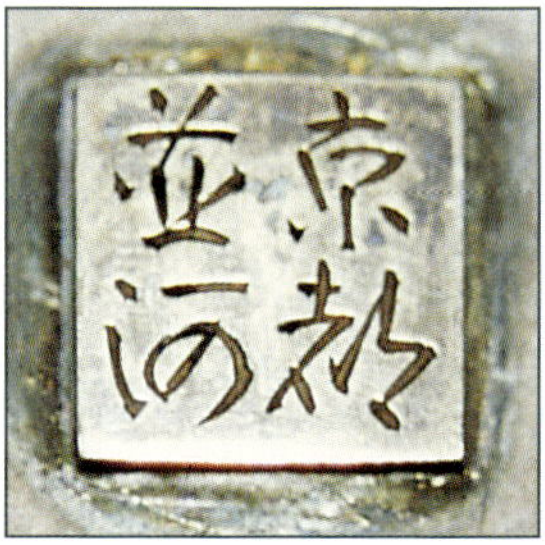

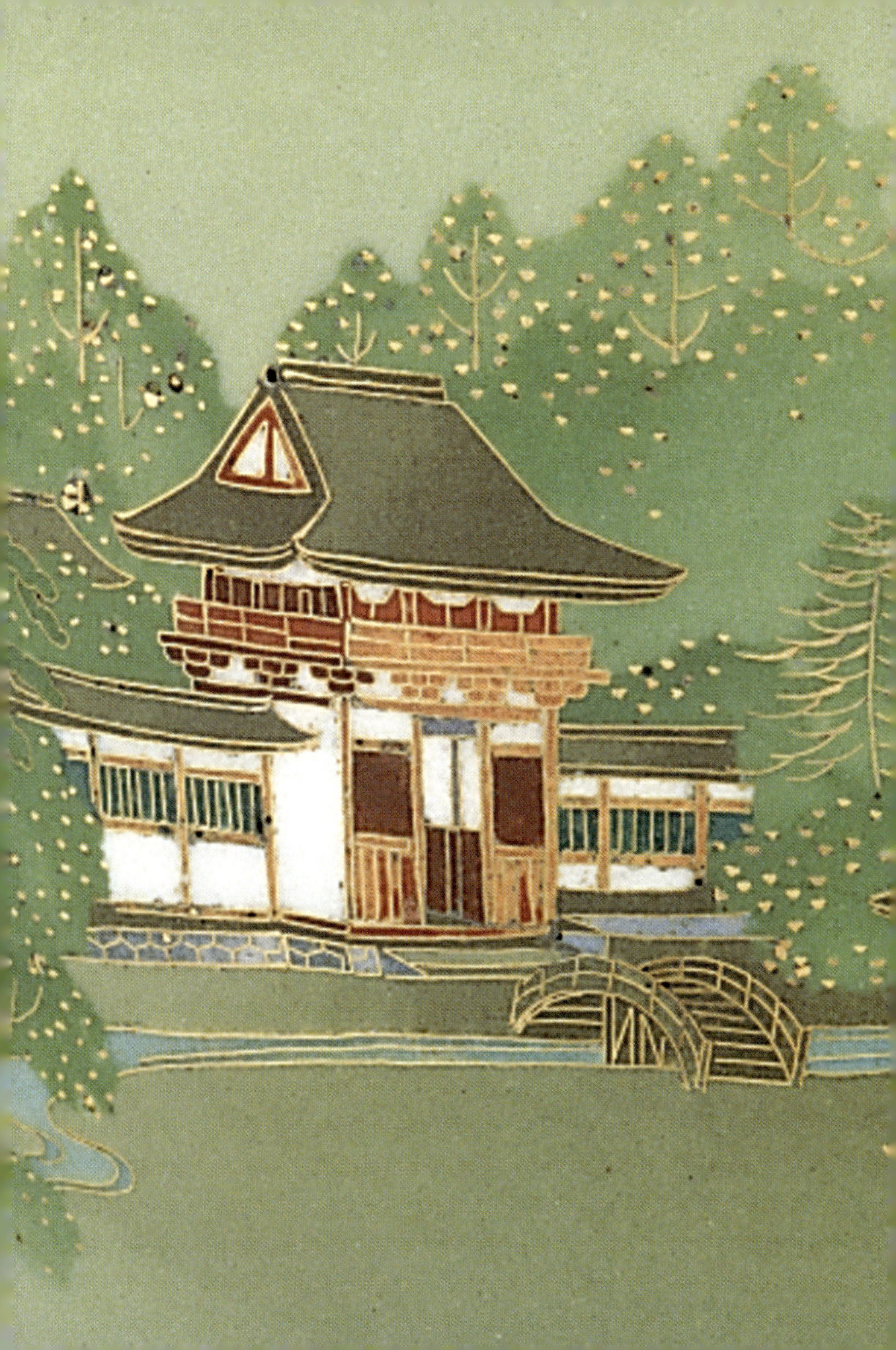

38 Vase

Cloisonné enamel
By Namikawa Yasuyuki
Signed:
c. 1910
H. 24.9 cm

Anonymous Fund 2002.177

Vase of almost cylindrical shape, widening at the base with a waterfall over rocks and plants mainly in sculpted silver wire on shades of blue enamel but with some *shakudō* wire and brown and green rocks and leaves. Engraved signature: *Kyōto Namikawa*.

Shortly before he retired in 1915, Yasuyuki was becoming too old-fashioned for the changing market in cloisonné; standards in general were dropping, as a cheaper product, superficially of fine quality, but actually much less well-made, filled an increasingly international mass market. Yasuyuki refused to compromise, and during this period produced some of his finest and most monumental work. The waterfall vase shows his mastery of the subtle use of both wire and of colour and of the adaptation of decoration to form. He had won innumerable gold and silver medals at almost all of the great International Expositions, and in 1896 he had been nominated an 'Imperial Artist'.

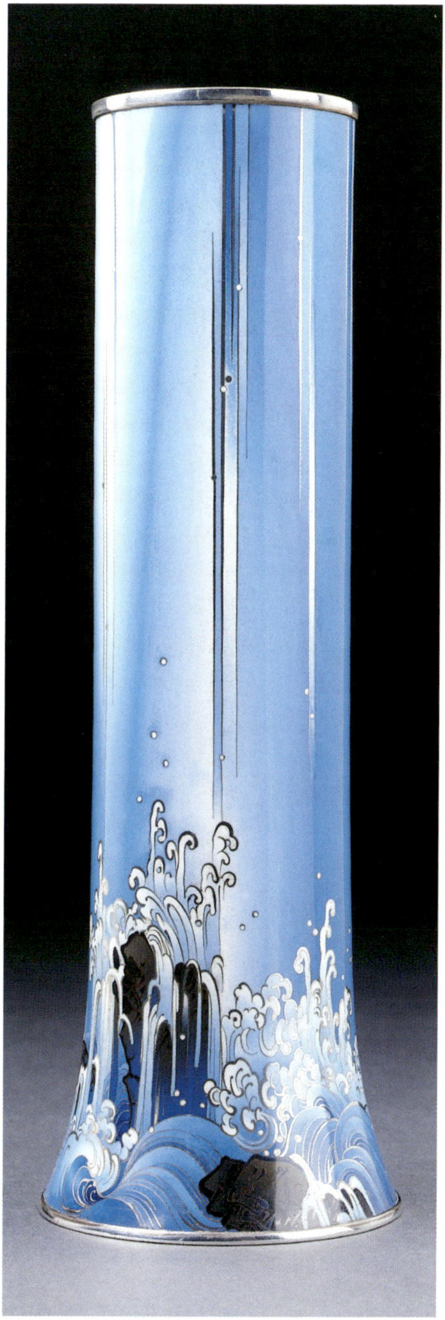

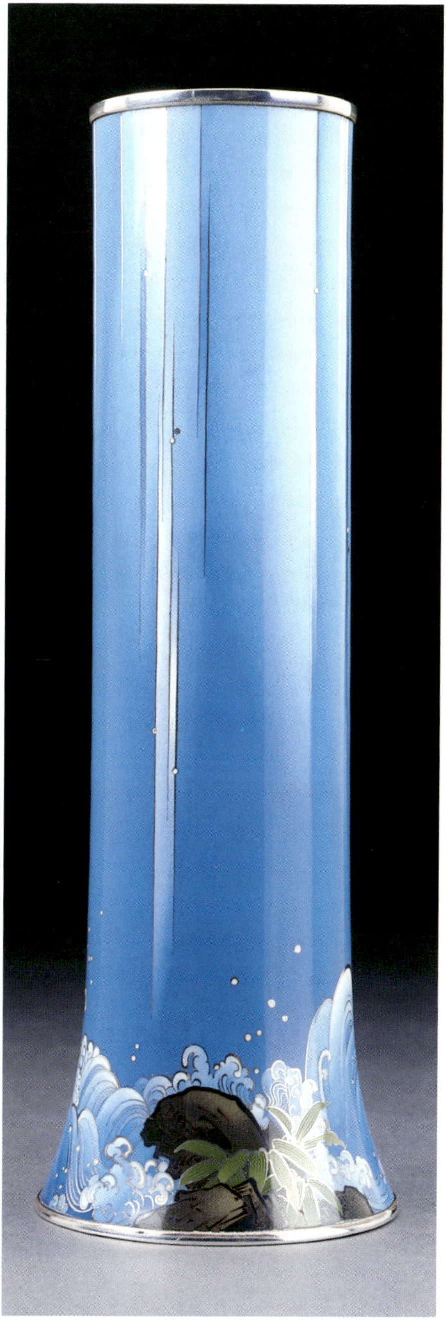

39 Vase

Cloisonné enamel
By Andō Jūbei (attributed to Hayashi Kodenji)
c. 1900
H. 25.2 cm Story Fund 1987.12

Cloisonné enamel vase the body worked in gold wire with sparrows and bamboo on a midnight blue ground, the borders worked in silver wire with flowering *kiri* (*Paulownia*) and scrolls. Applied seal mark of *Andō Jūbei*.

Although signed by the Andō factory mark, we believe that this vase, for stylistic reasons, was probably actually made by Hayashi Kodenji (1831–1915), a highly skilled enameller who worked at one time or another either on his own (there are pieces signed by him) or with other factories, or with the Andō factory; there are pieces signed by both Andō and Hayashi, but that not being the case here does not invalidate our attribution. A jar and cover of very similar work in gold wire in the Khalili Collection (Impey and Fairley, 1994, vol. 3 no. 62) is signed by Hayashi alongside the Andō mark.

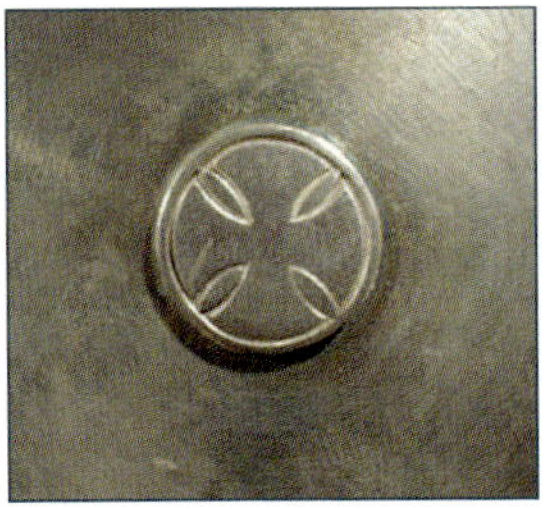

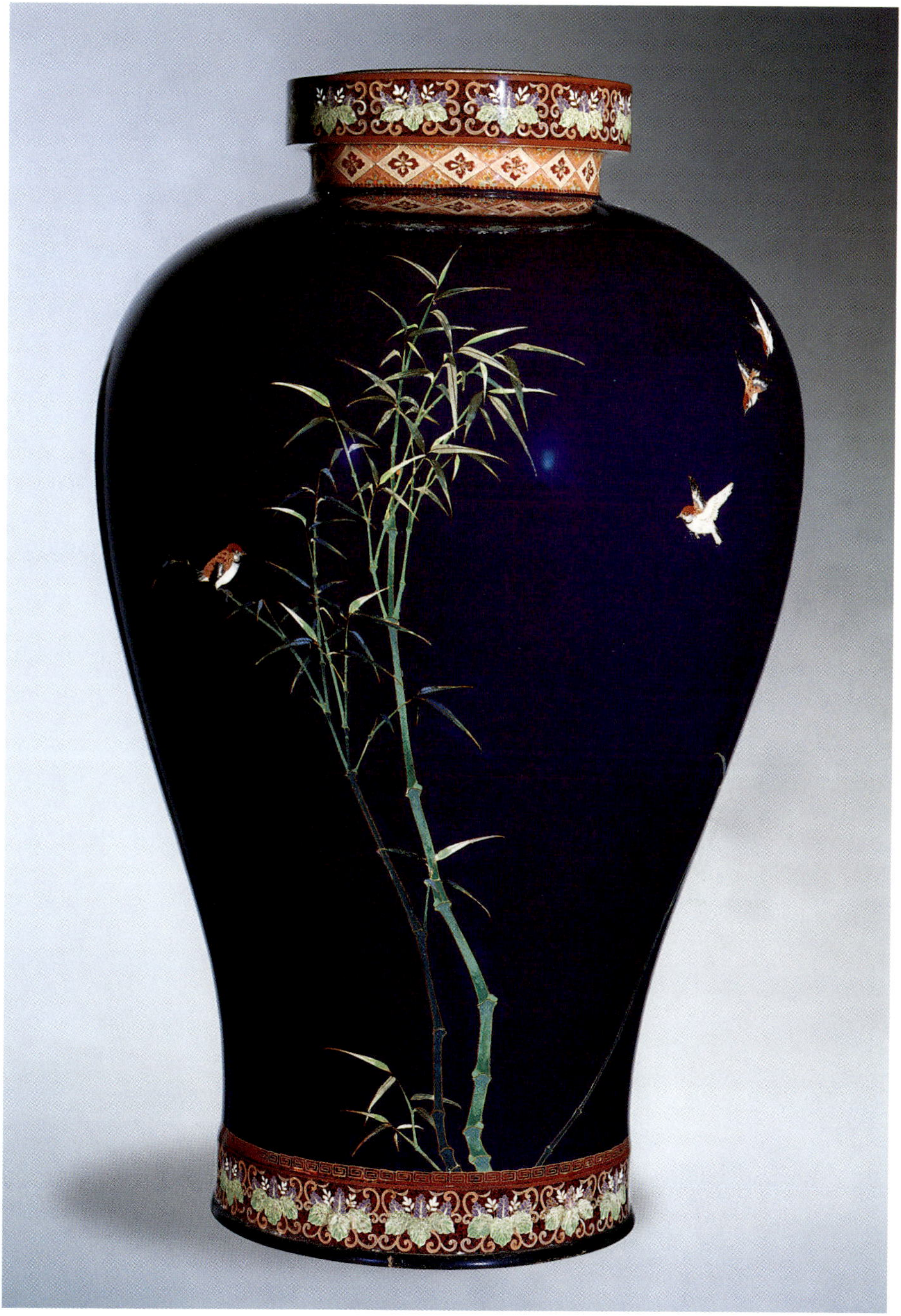

40 Vase

Cloisonné enamel
By Andō Jūbei
Signed
c. 1900
H. 41.4 cm

Reitlinger fund 1998.214

Baluster shaped vase of cloisonné enamel on a copper base. Decorated with chrysanthemums and a butterfly in *moriage* on a graduated beige/beige blue ground
Signed: seal mark of *Andō Jūbei.*

The Andō factory specialised in larger pieces of cloisonné; not the largest, but of considerable size. Eclectic in design, the factory kept up with demand and used most of the innovatory techniques as they appeared. By the first decade of the twentieth century, the factory was fully adapted to the Art Nouveau style, making large-scale pictorial patterns that conformed well to the shapes used, and with the frequent use of raised cloisonné enamel (*moriage*) that sounds almost like a contradiction in terms. One of the leading factories from the mid Meiji period, that factory is still working.

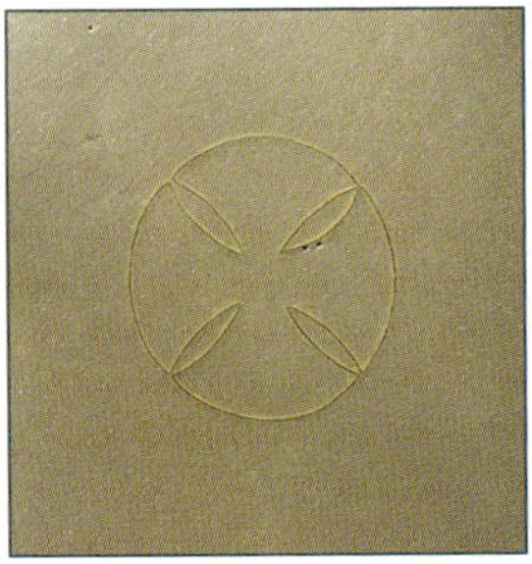

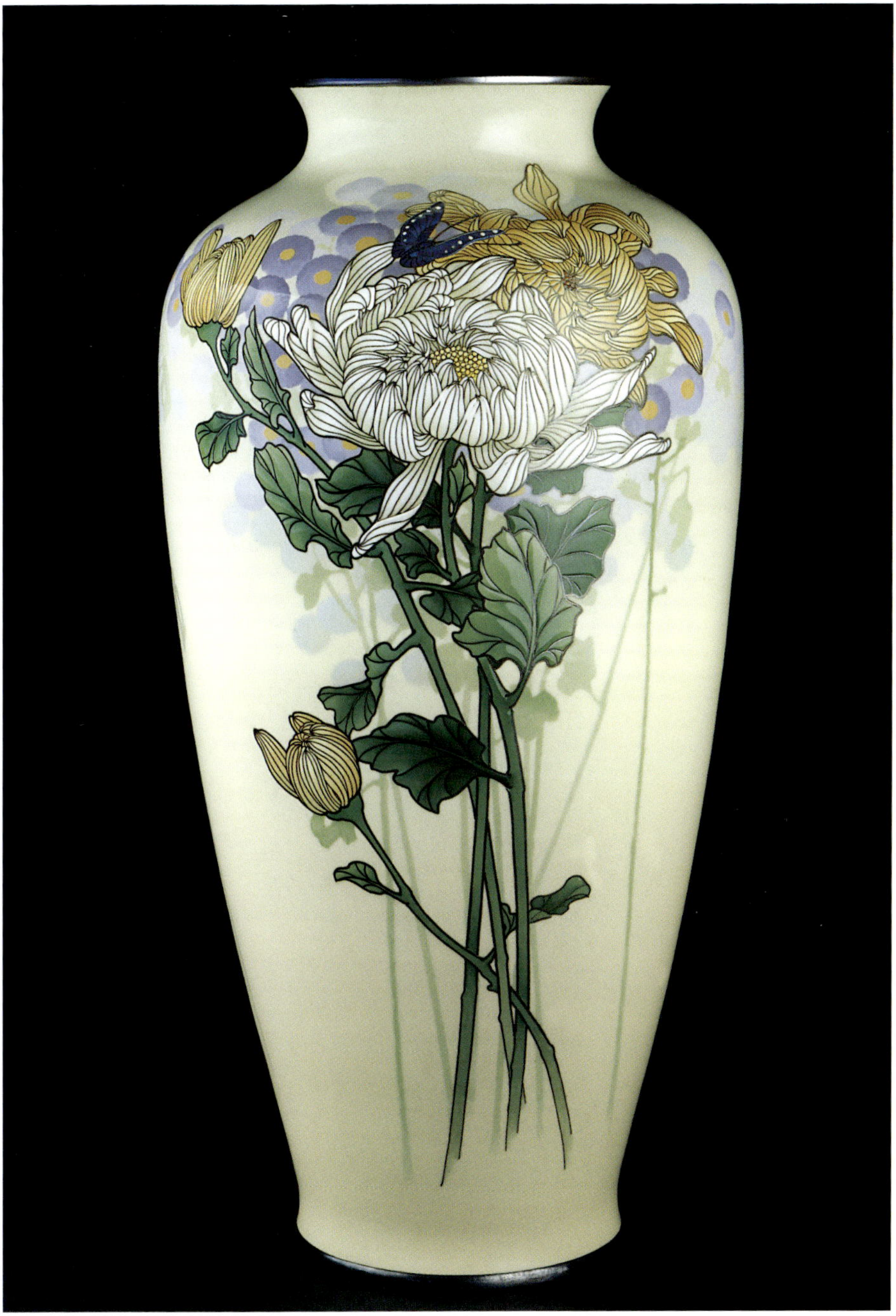

41 Vase

Cloisonné enamel
By Kumeno Teitarō
Signed
c. 1905
H. 21.6 cm

Story Fund 1999.104

Tall, slender vase with trumpet mouth. A gold dragon amid swirling waves encircles the body of green and pink enamels. A collar around the base of the neck incorporates the pearl, chased by the dragon. Stamped seal; *Kume.*

A *tour de force* of the later cloisonné techniques, this sculptural vase in gold and graded colour enamels has a pair now in a private collection. This is almost a culmination point in the making of cloisonné, it could hardly get further from its origins than this. Unusually, this vase was made in two pieces, with a collar around the neck as a join.

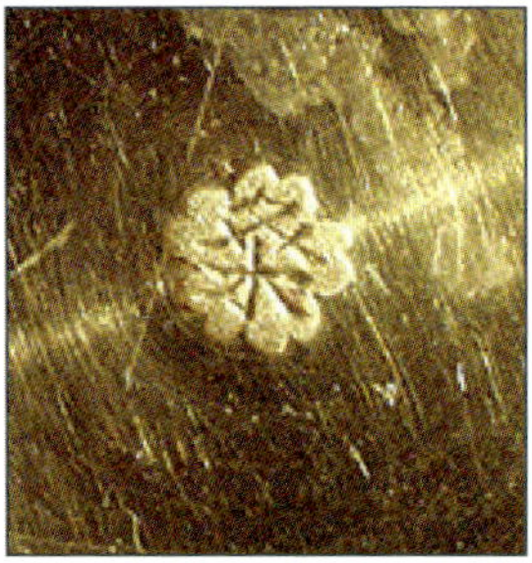

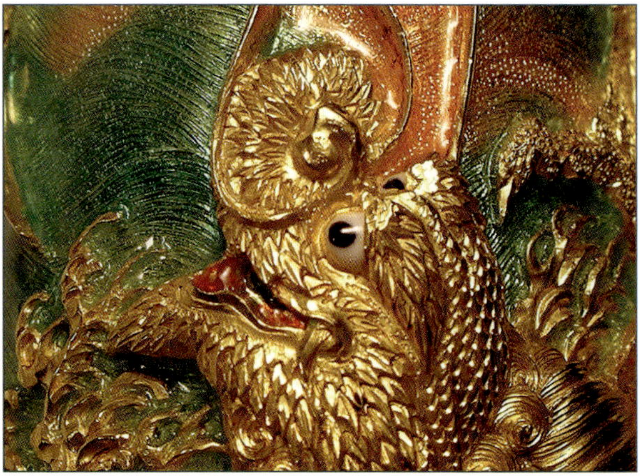

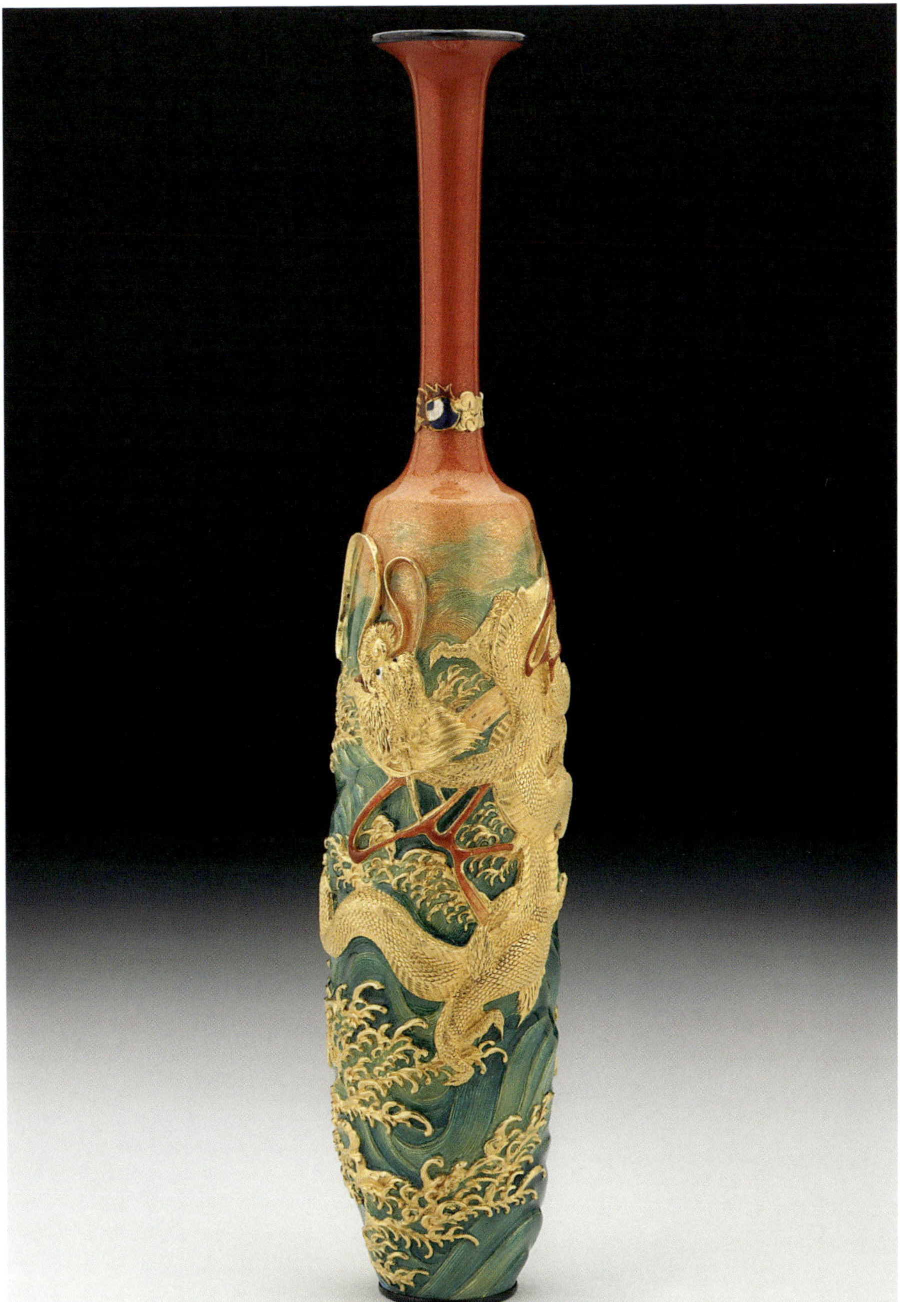

42 Vase

Cloisonné enamel
Attributed to Gonda Hirosuke
Unsigned
c. 1900
H. 34.9 cm Story Fund 1994.127

Cloisonné enamel baluster vase with a large spray of purple, pink and white magnolias on a buff ground.

This vase is almost identical to a pair exhibited by Gonda Hirosuke in 1900 at the Exposition Internationale in Paris, and illustrated in the catalogue (unnumbered and unpaginated) allowing us to be certain of our attribution. The conformation of the design to the shape demonstrates that not all Japanese crafts deserved the slating they received at that exhibition (see the Kinkōzan vase, no. 19).

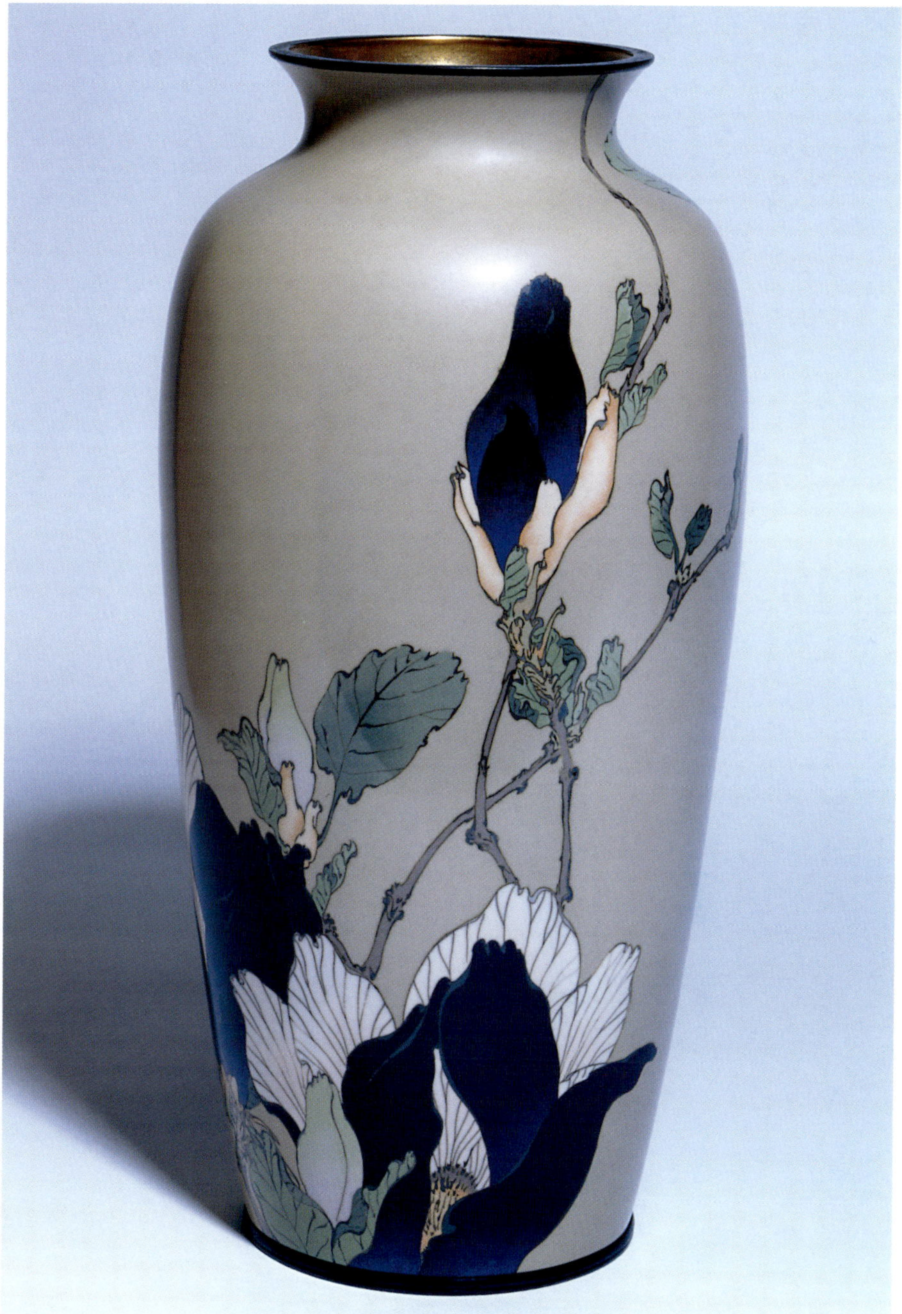

43 Vase

Cloisonné enamel
Plique-à-jour
Unsigned
1900–1910
H. 12.4 cm

Story Fund 1990.5

Plique-à-jour baluster-shaped vase decorated with chrysanthemums in coloured enamels against a translucent pale green background. The base and the upper rim mounted in silver.

Cloisonné enamel from which the supporting background has been removed, thus rendering it transparent, is called *plique-à-jour*, (*shōtai-jippō* in Japanese). It is extremely fragile. This very difficult technique was invented in France and first came to the notice of the Japanese enamellers when it was seen at the Paris Exposition in 1900 by Andō Jūbei. He bought some pieces by Fernand Thesmar, and it was from these that Kawade Shibatarō is said to have learned the technique. The skill spread, and other makers were soon producing it, most notably Hattori Tadasaburō, but we are unable to attribute this unsigned piece.

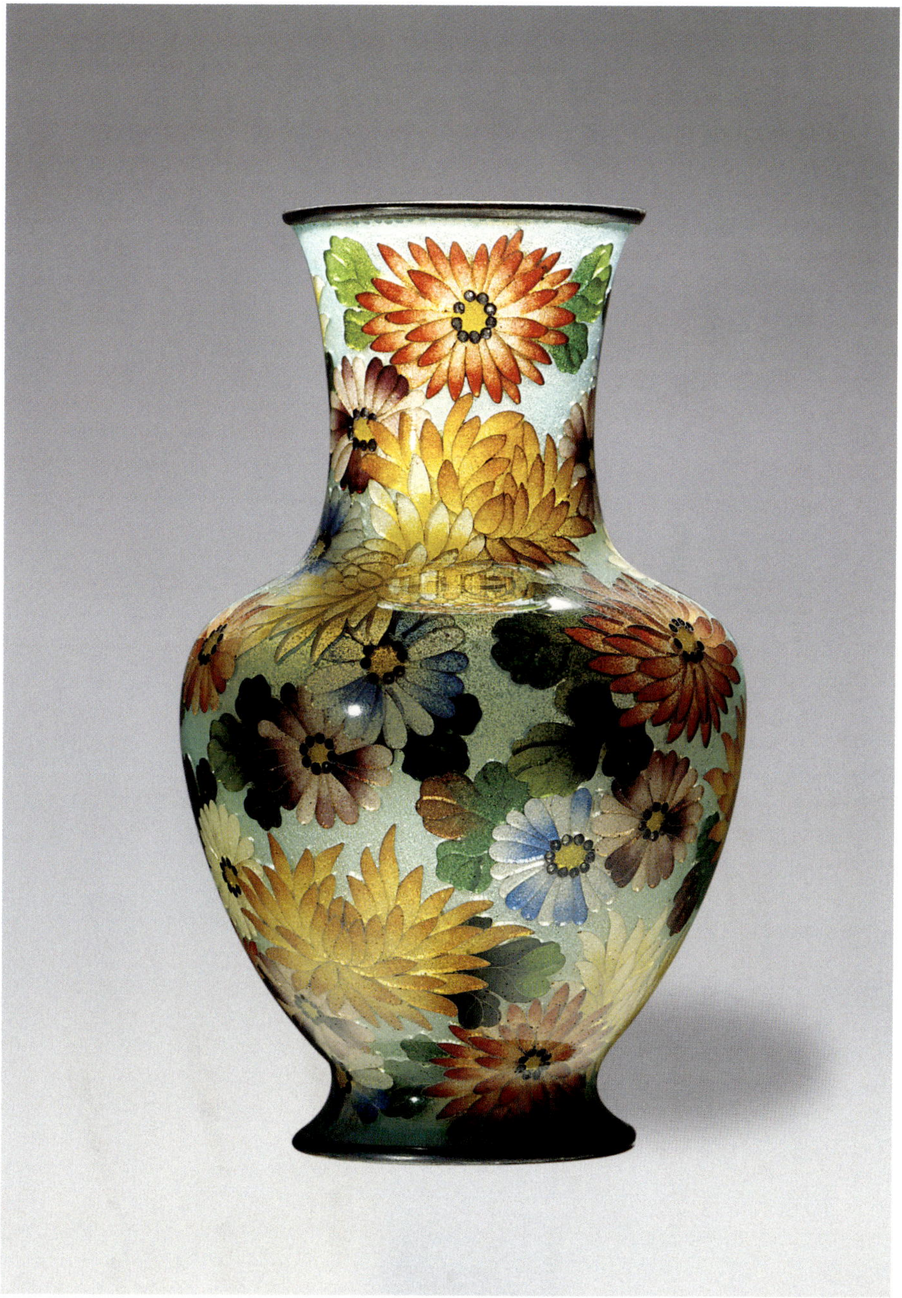

44 Tray

Cloisonné enamel
Attributed to Namikawa Sōsuke
The image signed by Watanabe Seitei
early 1880s
W. 29.6 cm: H. 19.7 cm Story Fund 2000.50

Rectangular tray with two sparrows, one holding a fruiting branch in its beak, perched on a bough, with a white ground surrounded by a foliate border. The reverse with clouds and stylised flowers on a turquoise ground. The tray unsigned; the image signed: *Seitei* with *kakihan*.

Namikawa Sōsuke (1847–1910) (no relation to Namikawa Yasuyuki) was more of an entrepreneur than an artist, though he did have a more-or-less consistent 'house style'. He specialized in the use of less and less visible wire, making his work look as much like a painting on porcelain as possible; indeed he both adapted the work of at least two painters on a regular basis, and produced cloisonné copies of famous historical paintings. Frequently he collaborated with the artist Watanabe Seitei (1851–1918) (see also nos. 46 and 47), whose signature would be found on the front of the work, while Sōsuke's would be found on the reverse. This tray is in Seitei's somewhat scratchy early style, contrasting with the slightly blander style of the following pieces.

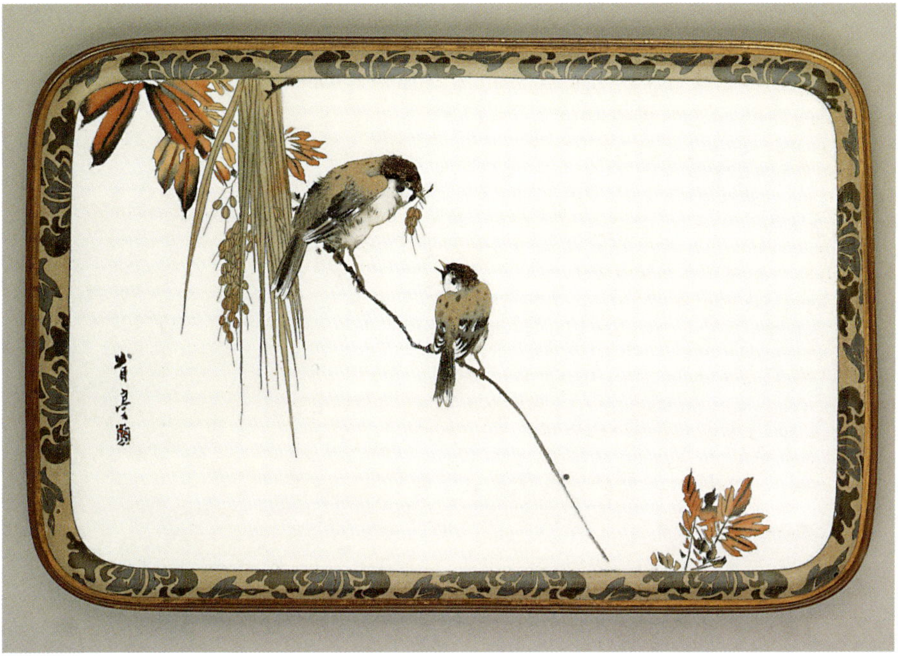

45 Vase

Cloisonné enamel
Attributed to Namikawa Sōsuke
Unsigned
early 1880s
H. 16.0 cm

Story Fund 1997.209

Baluster shaped vase with an overall design of stylised flowers against a white ground.

An unusual pattern-making design by Sōsuke who normally would have used such patterns only for borders. This is early for a white ground and it may well have been experimental.

Formerly in the collection of Michael Tomkinson (label on base), and included in 'A Japanese Collection, in two volumes made by Michael Tomkinson' and published in 1898, no. E 20.

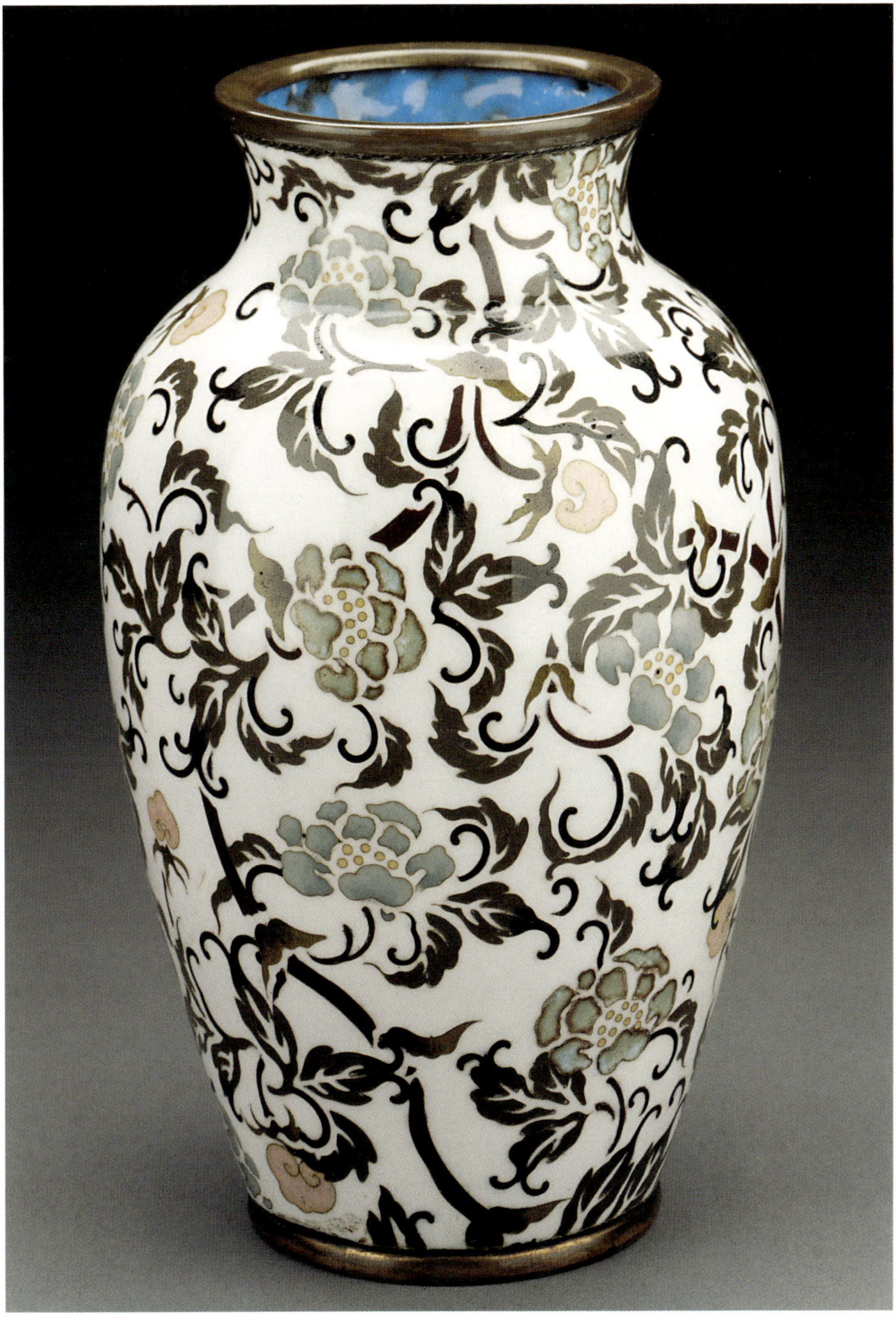

46 Tray

Cloisonné enamel
Attributed to Namikawa Sōsuke
The image signed by Watanabe Seitei
1885-1890
H. 29.2 cm Story Fund 1994.35

A white cockerel and hen with a dark mottled chick stand against a pale blue ground, within a foliate border. The reverse with different coloured shapes of a snowflake, cherry blossom and crescent moon on a turquoise ground. The tray unsigned; the image signed: *Seitei* with *kakihan*.

The wire is used here as emphasis; it makes part of the picture, but Sōsuke could well have dispensed with it if he had wished to; the wire is vital to the composition. Later he was to devise pictorial patterns where the wire is almost all invisible. In the Third National Industrial Exposition in 1890 he exhibited a pair of wooden screens with inset *shippō* panels imitating the work of a series of famous painters from the tenth to the nineteenth centuries, at least one of which had no visible wire.

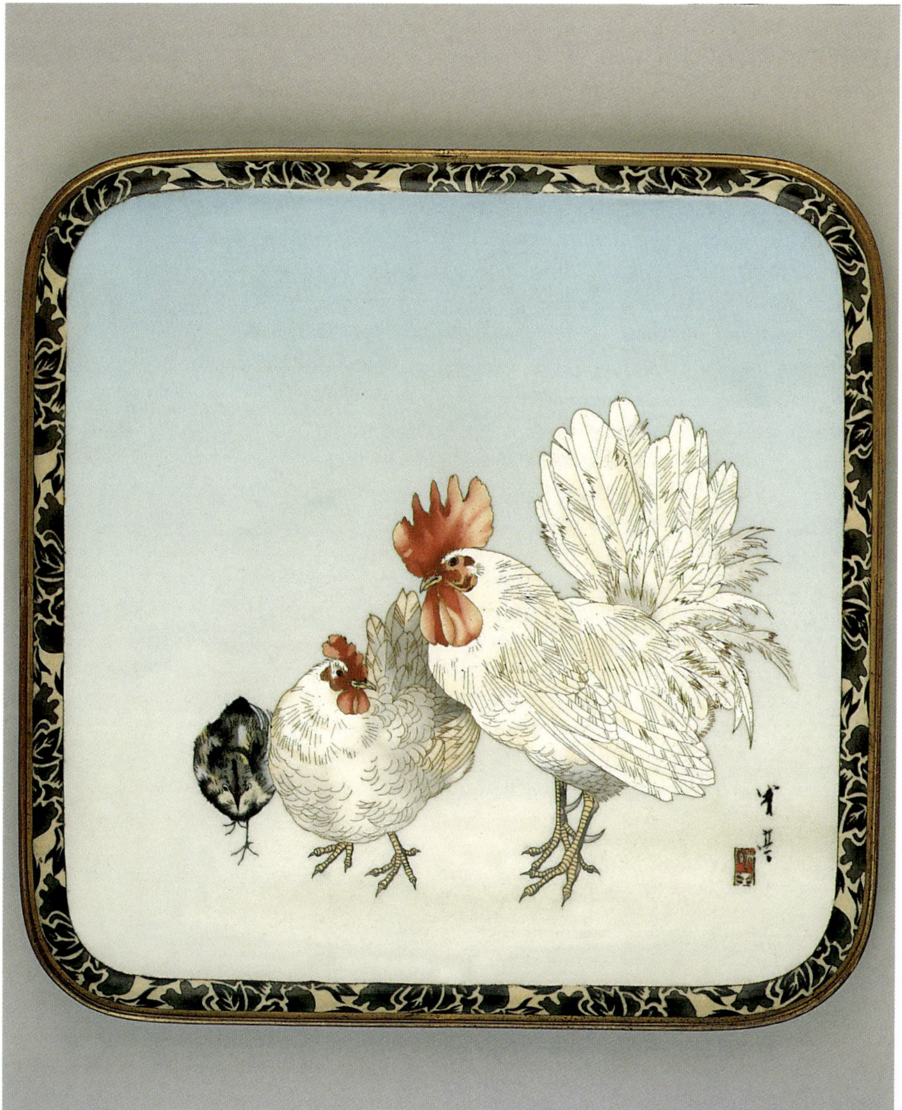

47 Tray

Cloisonné enamel
By Namikawa Sōsuke
The image signed by Watanabe Seitei
c. 1890
W. 30.0 cm — Story Fund 1990.4

Kidney-shaped tray with two pigeons in grey and white on a grey to beige ground. The reverse in matt brown enamel with various roundels. Silver and gold wire. The tray with the seal mark of *Sōsuke* on the reverse; the image signed: *Seitei* with *kakihan*.

The gradation of the coloured background was a feature much used by Sōsuke, in his desire to imitate painting. He had seen that his work was exhibited under the heading 'Fine art' in such exhibitions as the Japan-British in 1910, whereas that of his rivals, Namikawa Yasuyuki, Andō Jūbei and others who made no such attempt, were exhibited under 'Crafts'. This was a concept new to Japan, and new words had to be coined to express the concept, but it nevertheless satisfied some sort of desire for distinction in Sōsuke.

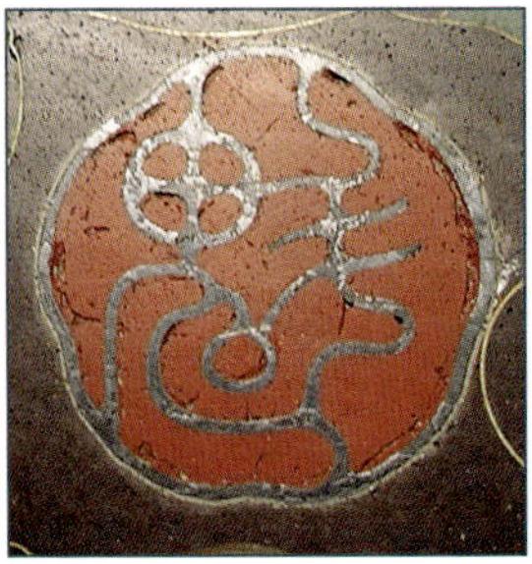

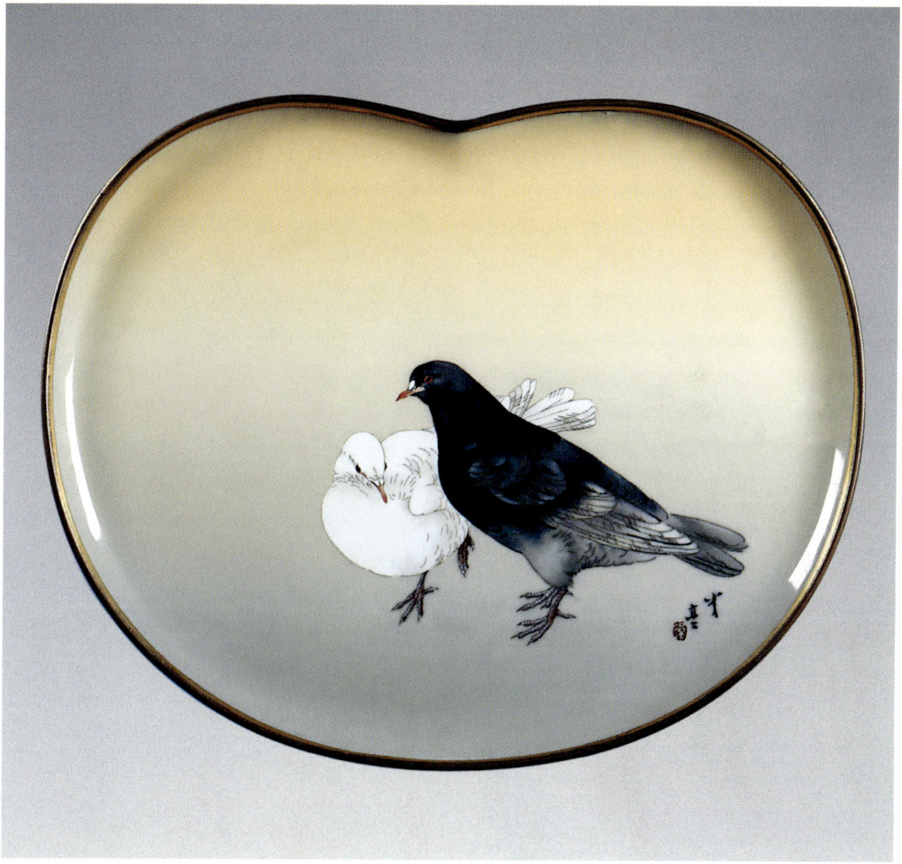

48 Incense box

Lacquer, metal and gold leaf
Unsigned
Early 20th century
D. 7.8 cm Gift of Richard Falkiner 1997.210

Incense box (*kōgō*) of black lacquer with two stylised bats and a crescent moon on the lid in gold leaf and *togidashi* with metal rims. The interior and base with sprinkled gold flakes on a black lacquer ground (*nashiji*).

Stylization is a frequent feature of Japanese art; here two bats have been depicted almost as if they were as round as the moon against which they are silhouetted.

Lacquer was the Meiji period craft that was least affected by the new markets. The old established craft was, of course, developed by such men as Shibata Zeshin (1807–1891), but only to a minor extent; there were no sweeping changes as there were in, say, metal-work. Works such as this, not intended for sale to a foreign client, retain the high quality achieved by painstaking and slow work, while the decoration is in the finest tradition of *maki-e* ('sprinkled picture') technique. The wood core of this incense box probably weighs less than six grams.

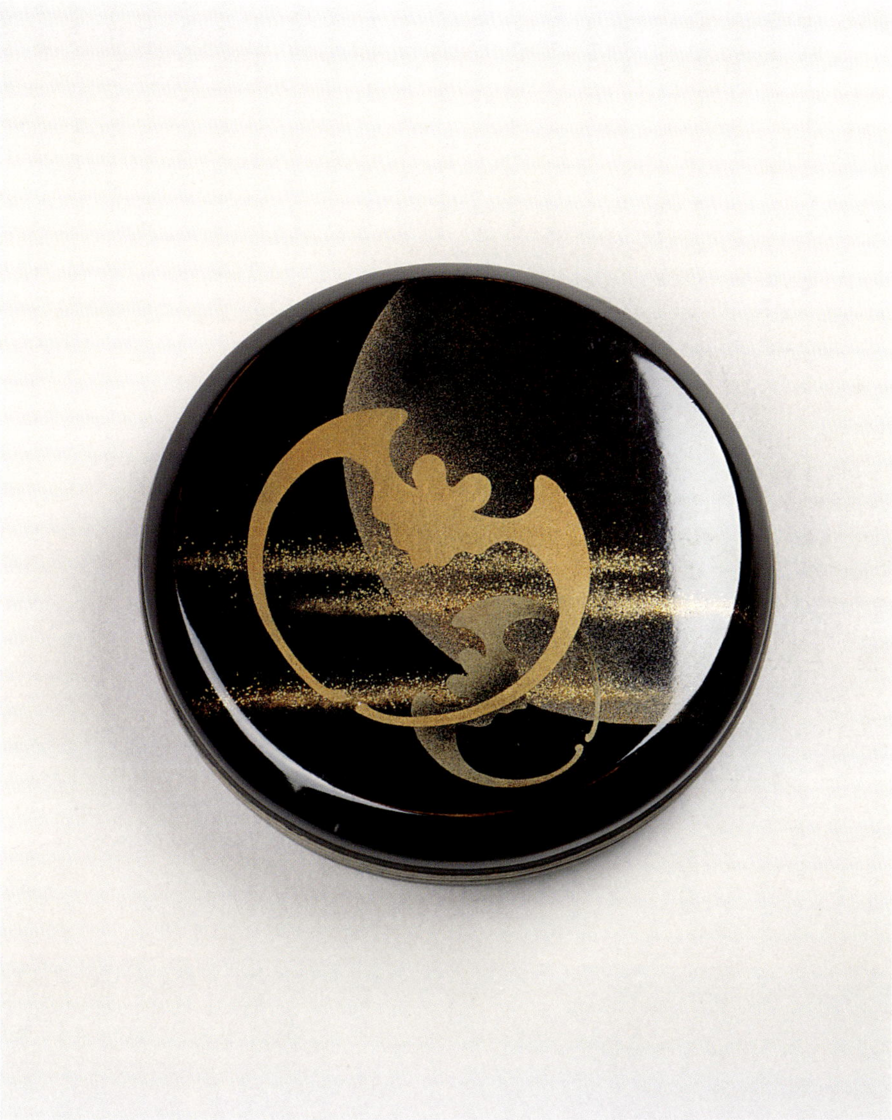

49 Box

Wood, lacquer and pearl-shell.
Unsigned
Late 19th/early 20th century
W. 15.3 cm: D. 11.8 cm: H. 5.9 cm

Gift of Sir Herbert Ingram 1956. 3337

Rectangular box with a design on the lid and sides of hydrangea leaves in raised lacquer (*takamaki-e*), the flower in high relief pearl shell. The canted corners of *nashiji* and the interior and base of densely sprinkled gold flakes (*nashiji*).

Crusted inlay of pearl-shell or other materials is an old Japanese technique, originally derived from Chinese models that were imported as early as the 6th century. But as with almost all 'borrowed' techniques, the Japanese developed their own way of doing things, by selection and rejection, until the results may far surpass the original models. The use of several techniques upon one object is almost a commonplace in Japanese work of the finest quality.

Bought by the Ingrams in Yokohama in June 1908 for 55 yen; quite a high price.

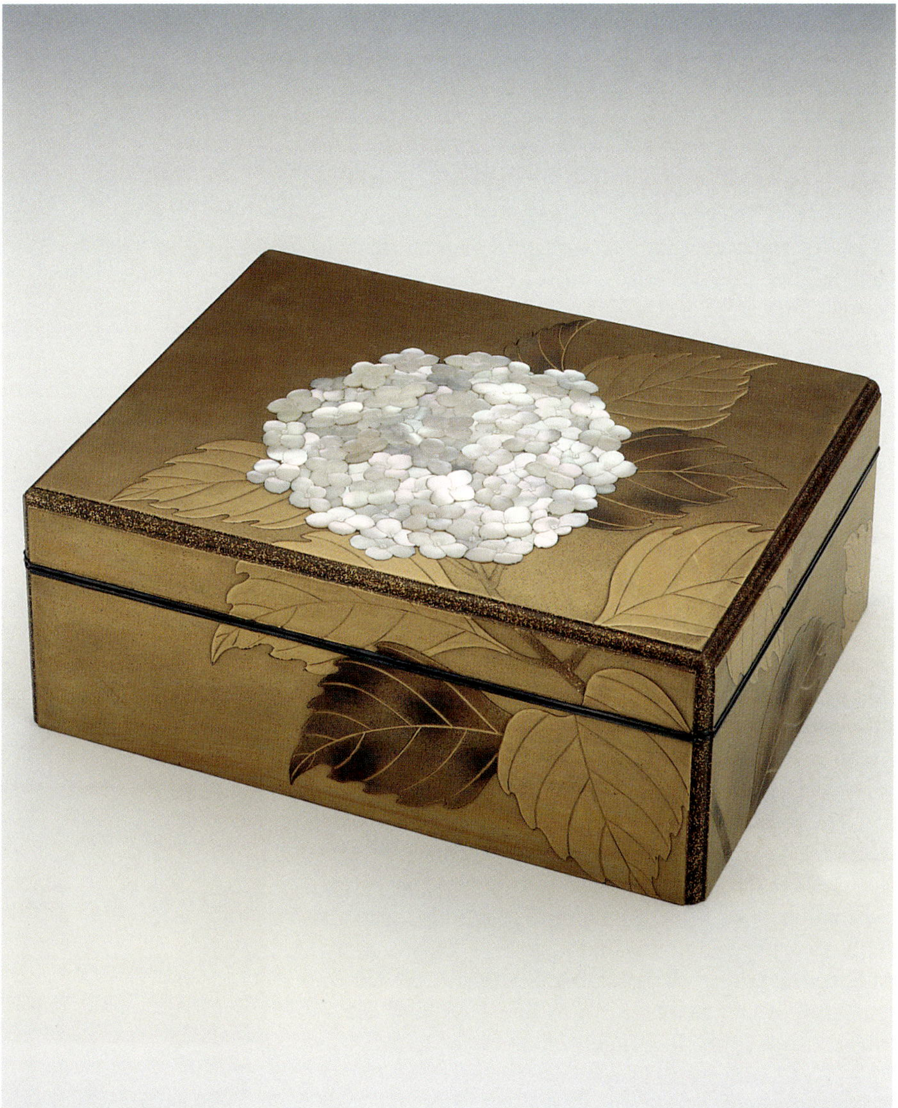

50 Pair of vases

Lacquer, cloisonné enamel, pearl shell, ivory and coral
By (Shibayama) Masaaki
Signed
c. 1890
H. 30.8 cm

Gift of The Khalili Family Collection of Japanese Art
in honour of Dr. Oliver Impey. 2000.5

A pair of Shibayama vases of hexagonal baluster shape in gold lacquer, the rims lined in silver, the neck with raised lacquer flowers and leaves on a matt gold ground and with cloisonné enamel collars. The body with ovoid panels foliated at the top, of inlays of flowers and birds in high relief in pearl-shell, coral and ivory reserved on a *hirame* ground, the feet of spear form. Signature: *Masaaki* (on pearl inset on base)

Very little is known of the makers of this, the Shibayama technique of inlays of a wide variety of materials into lacquer or ivory. The product of quite large workshops, the quality of inlay varies quite as much as does that of cloisonné; here the quality is very fine. Sometimes outworkers were used to supply standard cut-out figures of, say, mandarin ducks, which then could be incorporated into almost any picture; curiously, there seems to be no falling-off of quality in the case of such outworking, but no doubt this, too, varied.

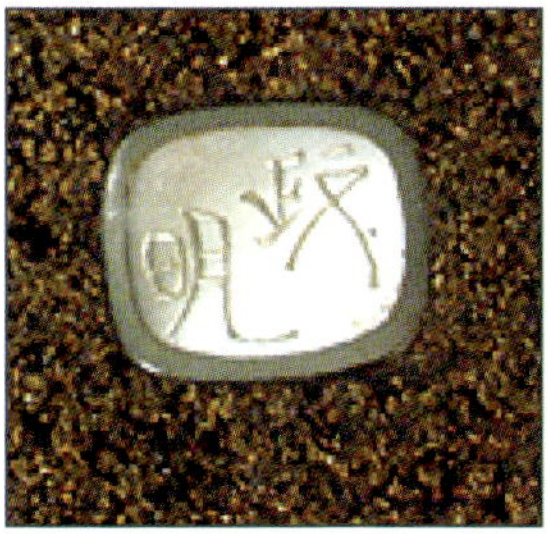

The technique may derive remotely from the work of Ritsuō (Ogawa Haritsu, 1663–1747), but does not seem to have been consolidated until the early Meiji period, when Shibayama Senzō won a prize in the First National Industrial Exposition in 1879. Little is known of the subsequent history of the Shibayama family, though the names of several members can be found on high quality objects made in the technique.

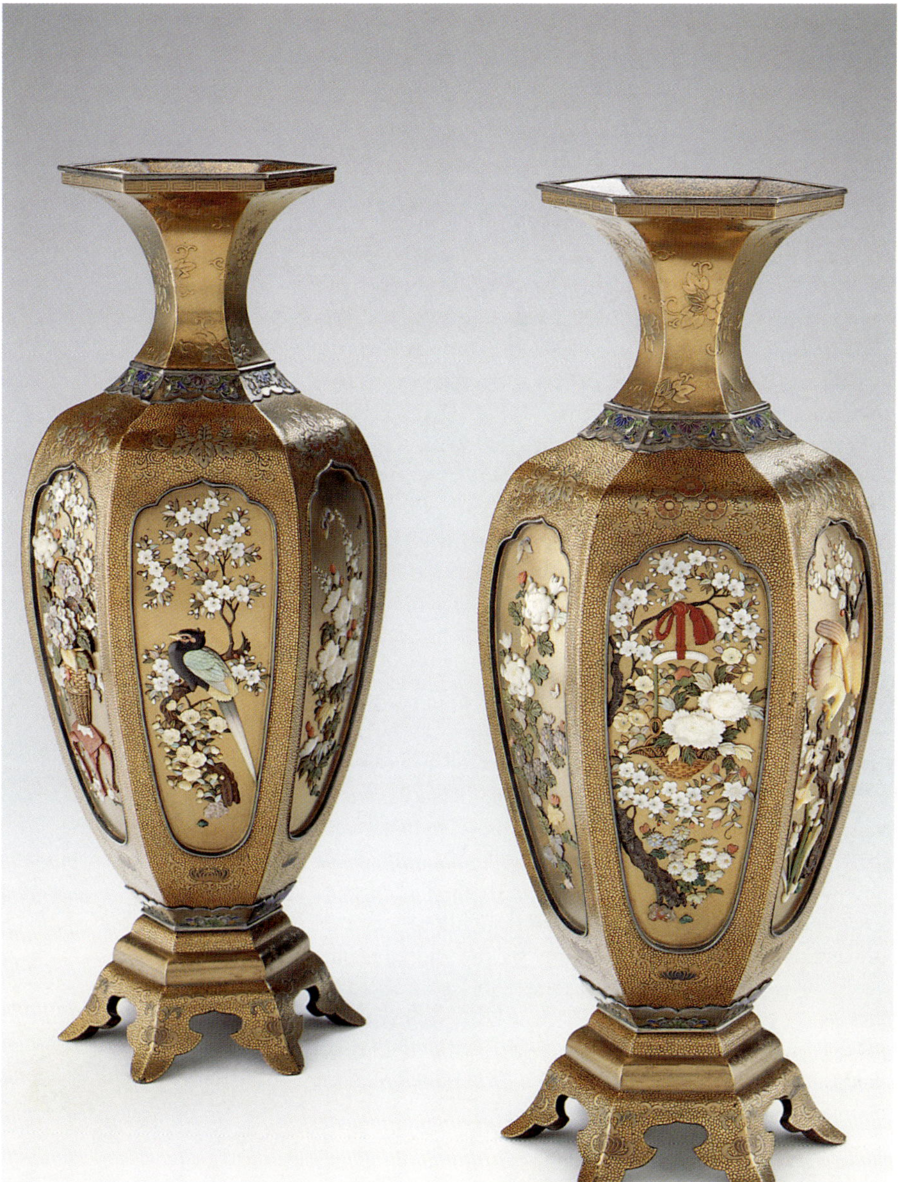

51 Inrō

Lacquer
By Shibata Zeshin (1807–91)
Two seals
Late 19th Century
L. 7.6 cm; W. 6.2 cm. X 600

Inrō with four compartments in red lacquer with a design of two Chinese inkcakes in black *takamaki-e* and red and gold *hiramaki-e*. The interior in *nashiji* and *fundame*. Two seals on the large circular inkcake read *Korenobu Zeshin.*

Shibata Zeshin was apprenticed at the age of eleven to the lacquer master Koma Kansai II (1767–1835) and subsequently studied painting with the Shijō school in Tōkyō under Suzuki Nanrei (1775–1844) and with Okamoto Toyohiko (1773–1845) in Kyōto. Despite his own skill for original design, Zeshin borrowed this one from Ogawa Haritsu, known as Ritsuō (1663–1747) and used variations of it on several of his lacquer pieces. His sparing use of gold and his experimentation with lacquers in imitation of metals, woods and pottery, are a feature of his work.

With the introduction of Western dress to Japan in 1872, the trouser pocket took the practical place of the inrō, which hung from the waist sash by means of a small toggle (*netsuke*). Artists, however, continued to make inrō, for their popularity with Western collectors provided a new market. After Zeshin exhibited in the Vienna Exposition in 1873, much of his work made its way into collections in America and Europe. By the end of his life he was as well known abroad as he was in Japan. In 1890, just one year before his death, he was honoured with the title *Teishitsu Gigeiin* (Imperial Artist), the first artist working with lacquer to receive it.

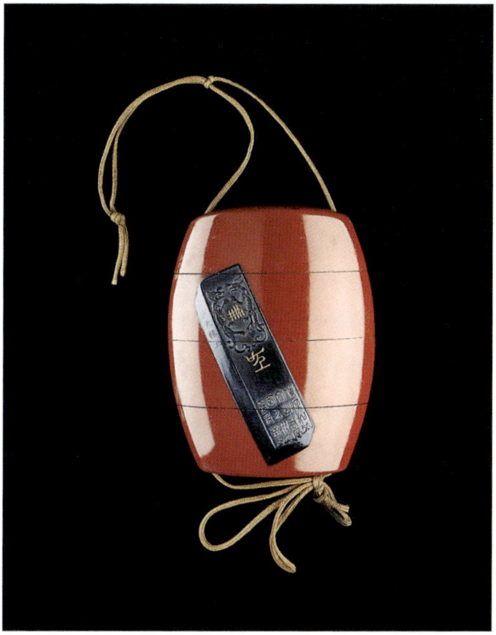

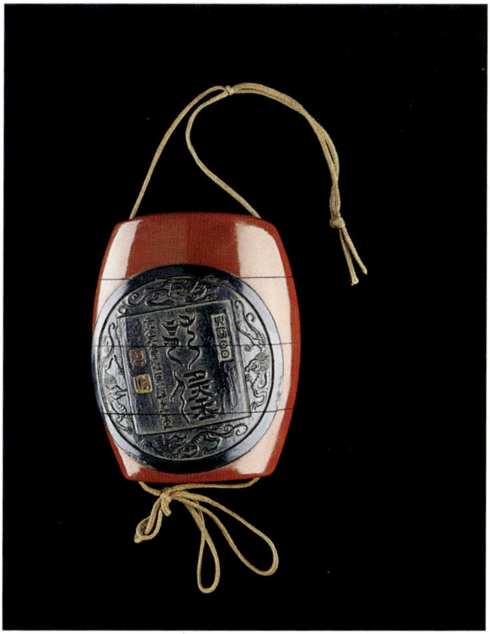

52 Netsuke

Ivory
By Ikkosai Kōjitsu
Signed Ikkosai Kōjitsu with kakihan
Mid-late 19th century
D. 5.7 cm. Barnett Bequest 2001.100

Manjū netsuke with a lively design carved in sunken relief of two of the Seven Gods of Good Fortune (*Shichifukujin*) posing as street entertainers. Daikoku, his mallet tucked into his belt, beats a drum as Ebisu, fan in hand, dances to the rhythm.

Ikkosai Kōjitsu (1833–1893) specialised in the carving of ivory *manjū* netsuke, after joining the Hōjitsu School in Tōkyō. The great Ansei earthquake and fire in Tōkyō in 1854 destroyed large numbers of netsuke and in order to replace them in a less time-consuming way, a circle of ivory was cut and the basic shape turned on a lathe. The carved decoration was then added by hand. Although the shape existed before, many of this type date from after the disaster. The name *manjū* refers to the shape of bean-cakes.

The Barnett bequest, of which this netsuke is representative, was given to the museum after the publication of *Japanese Netsuke in Oxford* in 1987.

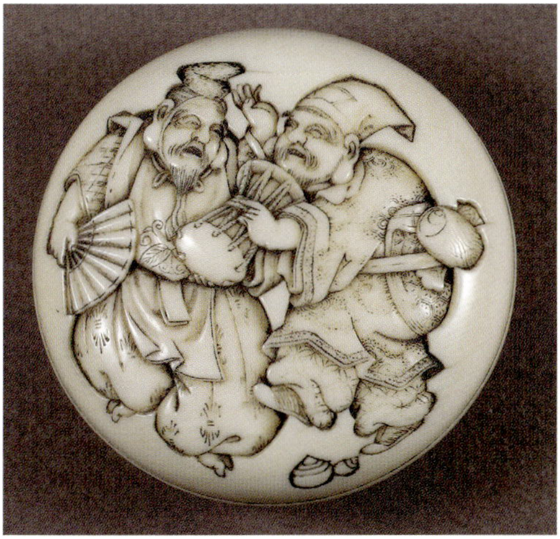

Glossary

Chōnin	Townsman or merchant
Daimyō	'Feudal' lord
Gō	Art name
Fundame	Matt gold lacquer ground made by sprinkling very finely ground gold powder
Hirame	Metallic particles, of graded sizes, used in lacquer decoration
Kakihan	Artist's written seal or 'logo'
Kyō-yaki	Pottery made in Kyōto
Maki-e	'Sprinkled picture' technique in which the design is built up by repeated alternating applications of coats of lacquer and metallic dust
Mizusashi	A cold-water container used in the tea ceremony
Moriage	Raised decoration
Nanga	Lit. 'Southern painting' – Edo period (1600–1868) Japanese painting school derived from Chinese models
Nashiji	Technique of employing regular flattened flakes of gold dust buried in transparent lacquer – 'aventurine'
Oshi-e	Padded fabric picture
Oyatoi gaijin	A foreigner employed by the Japanese government to develop Japanese industry and art industry
Nunome-zōgan	Decorative application of metal sheeting (generally of gold or silver) where the iron ground is first cross-hatched and the metal burnished on
Shakudō	Dark pickled metal alloy of copper and gold

Shippō Lit. 'Eight Treasures' – cloisonné

Shibuichi Pickled alloy of silver and copper

Sayagata Repeating background pattern of broken crosses or 'swastikas'

Takamaki-e 'Sprinkled relief design' – technique in which motifs are built up using lacquer or lacquer mixed with other materials, prior to sprinkling with metal powders

Teishitsu gigeiin Title: Imperial artist

Togidashi Technique in which the design in metal powders sprinkled over damp lacquer, is permitted to harden, then entirely covered with lacquer and finally after hardening, polished with abrasives to re-expose the design

Tsuba Sword guard

Tsutsugaki A method of resist dyeing, in which areas of cloth are painted with starch paste, applied through a bamboo tube (tsutsu), to protect them from the dye

Select bibliography

Baekland, Frederick, *Imperial Japan; the art of the Meiji Era* (1868–1912), Cornell, 1980.

Coben, Lawrence and Dorothy Ferster, *Japanese cloisonné*, New York and Tōkyō, 1982.

Earle, Joe, *Splendors of Meiji; masterpieces from the Khalili Collection*, St Petersburg, Florida, 1999. Catalogue of an exhibition held at Wilmington, Delaware.

Hahn, Gisela, *Meiji ceramics; the art of Japanese export porcelain and Satsuma ware, 1868–1912.* Stuttgart, 2004.

Harris, Victor, *Japanese Imperial Craftsmen; Meiji Art from the Khalili Collection*, London, 1994. Catalogue of an exhibition held in the British Museum.

Hida Toyojiro, *Kiritsu Kōshō Kaisha kōgei sitazushu; Meiji no yushutsu kōgei zuan. [A collection of designs and preparatory drawings for decorative arts for the First Industrial Manufacturing Company; designs for Meiji export wares]*, Kyōto, 1987.

Impey, Oliver, *Japanese Netsuke in Oxford from the Ashmolean Museum, Pitt Rivers and the Museum of the History of Science*. Ashmolean Museum, Oxford, 1987.

Impey, Oliver, *Reflections upon the Crafts of Meiji Period Japan with Reference to the Collection in the Ashmolean Museum*. Oriental Art, 1996, No. 3, p. 10–17.

Impey, Oliver and Malcolm Fairley, *The Dragon King of the Sea; Japanese Art of the Meiji Period from the John R. Young Collection*, Oxford 1991.

Impey, Oliver and Malcolm Fairley (eds.), *Meiji no takara, Treasures of Imperial Japan. Catalogue of the Nasser D. Khalili Collection of Japanese Art*. London, 1994, 8 vols.

Impey, Oliver and Malcolm Fairley, *Treasures of Imperial Japan; ceramics from the Khalili Collection*, London, 1994. Catalogue of an exhibition held at the National Museum of Wales, Cardiff.

Pollard, Clare, *Master Potter of Meiji Japan; Makuzu Kōzan (1842–1916) and his Workshop*, Oxford, 2002.

Ponting, Herbert, *In Lotus-Land Japan*, London, 1910.

Schaap, Robert (ed.), *Meiji; Japanese art in transition*, The Hague, 1987.

Tōkyō National Museum, *Chōsa kenkyū hōkokusho. Onchi zuroku, (Research report on the Onchi zuroku)*. Tōkyō, 1997.

Tōkyō National University of Fine Arts and Music, *Kōgei. A view of a century of modern Japanese crafts*, Tōkyō, 2004. Catalogue of an exhibition held in the University Art Museum.

Yoshida Mitsukuni (ed.), *Kyō-shippō monyō shu, [Collected designs for Kyōto cloisonné enamel]*, Kyōto, 1981. (Selected drawings by Nakahara Tessen).